taste of
honey

OTHER BOOKS BY MARIE SIMMONS

Fresh & Fast Vegetarian

Things Cooks Love (Sur La Table)

Soups and Stews (Williams-Sonoma)

Fig Heaven

Essentials of Healthful Cooking (Williams-Sonoma)

The Amazing World of Rice

Cookies (Williams-Sonoma)

The Good Egg

Puddings A to Z

Pancakes A to Z

Muffins A to Z

Bar Cookies A to Z

Holiday Celebrations (Williams-Sonoma)

Fresh & Fast

Lighter, Quicker, Better (with Richard Sax)

The Light Touch Cookbook

Rice: the Amazing Grain

365 Ways to Cook Pasta

Italian Light Cooking

Better by Microwave (with Lori Longbotham)

Good Spirits (with Barbara J. Lagowski)

taste of
honey

*the definitive guide to tasting
and cooking with 40 varietals*

marie simmons
photography by meg smith

**Andrews McMeel
Publishing, LLC**
Kansas City • Sydney • London

Andrews McMeel Publishing, LLC
an Andrews McMeel Universal company
1130 Walnut Street, Kansas City, Missouri 64106
www.andrewsmcmeel.com

ISBN: 978-1-4494-2754-2

13 14 15 16 17 SHO 10 9 8 7 6 5 4 3 2 1

Library of Congress Control Number: 2013930080

Design: Julie Barnes
Photography: Meg Smith
Digital/Photo Assistant: David Escalante and Katie Newburn
Food Stylist: Nani Steele
Prop Stylist: Christine Wolheim

www.mariesimmons.com

ATTENTION: SCHOOLS AND BUSINESSES
Andrews McMeel books are available at quantity discounts with bulk purchase for educational, business, or sales promotional use. For information, please e-mail the Andrews McMeel Special Sales Department: specialsales@amuniversal.com

Permissions

"In Which Tiger Comes to the Forest and Has Breakfast" by A. A. Milne, from The House at Pooh Corner by A. A. Milne, copyright 1928 by E. P. Dutton, renewed 1956 by A. A. Milne. Used by permission of Dutton Children's Books, a division of Penguin Group (USA) Inc.

"In Which We Are Introduced to Winnie-the-Pooh and Some Bees, and the Stories Begin" by A. A. Milne, from Winnie-the-Pooh by A. A. Milne, copyright 1926 by E. P. Dutton, renewed 1954 by A. A. Milne. Used by permission of Dutton Children's Books, a division of Penguin Group (USA) Inc.

The Poems of Emily Dickinson, Thomas H. Johnson, ed., Cambridge, Mass.: The Bellnap Press of Harvard University Press, copyright 1951, 1955, 1979, 1983 by the President and Fellows of Harvard College.

The Fourth Georgic by Virgil as translated in The Georgics of Virgil by David Ferry. Published by Farrar, Straus and Giroux

At the time of printing, every effort was made by the author to obtain all other permissions.

contents

acknowledgments

It takes many minds and multiple palates to make a cookbook. The primary instigators of this book are at the top of my thank-you list: Jean Lucas, my editor and the brain behind the idea of writing a cookbook to sort out the different honeys she encountered at her local farmers' market; Kirsty Melville, executive vice president and publisher at Andrews McMeel Publishing; and Carole Bidnick, my terrific agent, who suggested that I be the writer for this project.

Heartfelt thanks to the team at Andrews McMeel for the exquisitely designed pages of this book. Thank you to photographer Meg Smith, food stylist Nani Steele, and props from Christine Wolheim for stunningly beautiful work. You, along with your assistants, are all artists. A special thank-you to Rob Keller of Napa Valley Bee Company, beekeeper par excellence, for supplying honey, hives, and the beautiful honey bees for the photographs. Thank you also to my copy editor, Tammie Barker, for giving my work the polish it needed. A special thank-you to Emily Farris in advance of working with her on publicity. I am grateful to all of you.

Without the hard work of others, who spent hours and possibly years documenting the activities in the hive, keeping the bees healthy, working in labs and compiling historical records and references, and writing excellent books about bees and honey, the information in this book would be a bit puny. Several of you are mentioned in the text, and the rest can be found in the bibliography (page 178). I am grateful for your hard work, for it not only gave me knowledge and understanding but also fired my enthusiasm for honey, bees, and beekeepers to the point where I am now a bit of a bee—and honey—maniac.

May Berenbaum, a professor of entomology at the University of Illinois at Urbana-Champaign, deserves special mention because it was in one of her many books, *Honey, I'm Homemade*, that I found the precise answer to a nagging question, "What is honey?" Professor Berenbaum's excellent explanation—gratefully acknowledged here—helped me write a clear answer to this question. Thank you, Professor Berenbaum, for generously agreeing to vet portions of *A Taste of Honey* for me.

This book, because it is primarily a guide to honey varieties and a cookbook, translated into many happy—and somewhat sticky—hours spent in the kitchen tasting, testing, and tasting some more. Just days into the project I began calling my work space "the sticky kitchen" and was tempted to change the title to *The Sticky Kitchen Cookbook*. Stickiness did little to deter from my ever-increasing excitement for the subject, however. I started out liking honey a lot and ended up loving it. I also fell in love with the bees.

In addition to the bees, I am grateful for the generous support and assistance with honey and bee sleuthing I received from colleagues, friends, and family. They are too numerous to mention here, so I will name just a few: Helene and Spencer Marshall, longtime Napa Valley beekeepers, for your kind hospitality; Matt Bennett, for bringing a frame with wax honeycomb, dripping with raw honey, from his wife Ashley's beehive to a honey tasting I hosted for the San Francisco Professional Food Society; the National Honey Board, for its excellent, fact-filled website and support for this project; David Guas, honey aficionado and chef proprietor of Bayou Bakery in Arlington, Virginia, for introducing me to Appalachian sourwood at a tasting hosted by the honey board; Linda Sikorski and Juliana Uruburu of Market Hall Foods in Oakland, California, and The Pasta Shop in Berkeley, for more honey tasting and an insightful honey and cheese pairing experience; Brooke Jackson and Nancy Kux, for retesting a few recipes; Laura Brainin-Rodriguez, for nutritional wisdom, research, and friendship; Paula Hamilton and Pam Elder, dear friends and tireless researchers, for sending media alerts and honey factoids my way; Jenny and Hari Krishnan, neighbors and enthusiastic tasters; and Kathleen de Wilbur, Kathleen O'Neil, Debbie Rugh, and friends in my book club for keeping me sane.

And then there is my sweet and concerned family, who watched over me as I worked my way through this cookbook: John, my best friend and husband; Stephanie, our amazing daughter; Shawn, our thoughtful son-in-law; Seraphina, our beautiful and smart granddaughter; and Joseph, our adorable grandson, who at the age of three insisted that my honey chocolate cake needed chocolate icing, inspiring yet another honey recipe.

*To the honey bees
and their keepers:
Without you there
would be no honey*

> "Well," said Pooh, "it's the middle of the night,
> which is a good time for going to sleep. And tomorrow
> morning we'll have some honey for breakfast."
>
> —*The House at Pooh Corner*, A. A. Milne

introduction

Quite by coincidence, I ate honey for breakfast, too. But, unlike Pooh, I ate honey not by scooping it with a furry paw from the "hunny" jar, but dribbled onto a bowl of steaming oatmeal where it made a moatlike circle around a melting nugget of butter. Throughout my childhood, happiness was honey for breakfast. And when oatmeal wasn't on the menu I slurped at honey combined with melted butter dripping from the nooks and crannies on a toasted English muffin and washed it down with honey-sweetened hot tea diluted with milk. These are still some of the ways I love the taste of honey.

Of course, as a child I didn't know about different varieties of honey. Inside the jar on our breakfast table was most likely orange blossom or clover honey from the supermarket. But I also remember big jars of local honey purchased at farm stands along the country roads that wound through New York State's Hudson River Valley, where I grew up.

Today on the shelf in my pantry is a charming bear-shaped plastic bottle filled with honey. For years this iconic bear with the yellow cap was the only honey I used. During my years as a test kitchen editor at magazines, I made cakes, cookies, ice cream, and candy with honey of unspecified varieties. But my true honey epiphany—of sorts—came well into adulthood on a trip to Italy, where I was served a local chestnut honey spooned over a thin slice of oozy Gorgonzola dolce. I was enthralled with the combination. Honey and cheese? A classic pairing in the Lombardy region was a revelation. Sweet, salty, and bitter all congregated on my palate at the same time. My mouth was thrilled, and I was hooked (see Honey and Cheese Tasting, page 35).

Once home in my own kitchen, with a modest stash of Italian chestnut honey now a pantry staple, I began to take notice of the different varieties of honey in specialty shops and at farmers' markets. Today my collection of honey has labels that read like a travelogue: cranberry honey from Michigan, rosemary and black sage honey from the California Sierras, tupelo honey from Florida, oregano honey from Sicily, macadamia blossom honey from Hawaii, lavender honey from southern Oregon, and manuka honey from New Zealand.

As my honey collection grows, so does my repertoire of honey recipes. I still use honey in desserts, experimenting with the earthy taste of buckwheat, wild oak, avocado, or euca-lyptus honey in brownies and chocolate pudding, Sicilian lemon or orange blossom honey in panna cotta, star thistle honey in fruit sorbets, and lavender or tupelo honey in whipped cream. But it is the exploration of honey in savory dishes that intrigues me most.

For a sweet hit in savory recipes I proceed with caution, substituting clover or orange blossom honey for the sugar in a favorite recipe, Cold Chinese Noodles with Spicy Honey Peanut Sauce (page 105), and then moving on with each success to other recipes, adding a couple of spoonfuls to Stir-Fried Lamb, Japanese Eggplant, Red Bell Pepper, and Moroccan Spices (page 94), Chicken Stewed with Tomatoes, Green Olives, and Orange (page 88), and Shredded Cabbage with Creamy Toasted Cumin, Honey, Lime, and Jalapeño Dressing (page 112).

With every triumph I become bolder, taking notice of the nuances in flavors when a robustly flavored dark or amber honey is substituted for a light-colored, mild-tasting orange blossom honey. Bolstered by these experiences, I sort my honey collection into two categories, light or mild tasting and dark or more robust tasting (see The Colors of Honey, page 11). Now as I cook I can more readily find the honey best suited to the flavor profile of a recipe (see Cooking with Honey, page 37).

As my honey journey progressed I became fascinated—almost obsessed—with the subject. Cooking with different varietals is the topic of this book, but it is impossible to use honey every day, amass a collection of close to 100 jars of honey, and meet beekeepers and honey experts without growing admiration for the source of this golden gift from Mother Nature: the honey bee.

what is honey?

Honey is made by honey bees from the nectar of flower blossoms. The nectar is mostly water with some sugars. Converting nectar to honey isn't simple, but the honey bees do an astounding job. Here is a synopsis of what essentially happens: Within the nectar is a complex sugar (sucrose) that is broken down by an enzyme in the honey bee's saliva to the simple sugars: fructose and glucose. By repeated regurgitation (drop by drop from the bee's special honey tummy) and evaporation (by fanning its wings once the nectar is deposited in the honeycomb for curing), the water in the nectar is reduced, thereby thickening the honey and making it unable to ferment.

Meanwhile, another enzyme in the bee's saliva produces gluconic acid, which prevents microbial growth, and hydrogen peroxide, which acts as a sterilizing agent in honey. I know we like to think that honey is pure and unprocessed. It is in terms of human interference, but that is because the honey bees, with the help of Mother Nature, do the deed entirely on their own. Magical, isn't it?

> "Honey that's borne upon the winds of heaven,
> A gift of the high gods, is now my tale."
>
> —Virgil

the life of bees

If nothing else, the story of honey and how it is made will make it perfectly clear that the honey bee is brilliant.

Fossils indicate that bees have been around for perhaps 50 million years, which is when the first primates were appearing in Africa and South America. As one can imagine, bees, like the primates, have evolved over time.

The bee as we know it, *Apis mellifera*, or the European honey bee, was introduced to North America with settlers in the 1600s. It is this bee, and its subspecies, that produces most of the honey consumed today.

This wee little insect with amazing powers thrives in such a complex community that once we begin to grasp even just a small part of what it takes to produce honey we surely never will take honey bees—or honey—for granted.

Bee Society

- A bee colony consists of one queen, several hundred male drones, and 30,000 to 80,000 workers, all female.

- Bees are born into one of these groups and remain there for life. There is no such thing as climbing the social ladder in the bee community. Their efforts are for the common good.

- The queen, grown from larvae specially fed by the workers to be sexually mature, lays up to 3,000 eggs a day to keep the colony well populated. There is typically only one queen per hive at a time. When she stops laying eggs, she is replaced by a young queen that the workers groomed for the job.

- When the new queen is ready to take her virgin flight, the drones are attracted to her and mate with her in flight, depositing several million sperm cells. That's enough to last her lifetime, which can be two to five years.

- The sole responsibility of the drones—the only males in the colony—is to mate with the queen. Compared with the others in the bee community, they come off as lazy louts. The drones die when they mate, giving their lives for the good of the colony.

- Although their size makes them appear scarier than the worker bees, drones do not have stingers.

- The responsibility of the workers changes as they mature. The oldest workers, the foragers, are assigned the task of finding food for the hive. Foragers make ten or more round trips each day from hive to blossoms sucking nectar and collecting pollen; some are dedicated pollen foragers and others are nectar foragers.

- On their return to the hive they can carry nectar and pollen equal to their body weight. It's exhausting work; their life expectancy is 2 to 3 weeks.

- Typically bees will travel within a 2- to 3-mile radius of their beehive to collect nectar and pollen, both essential to the life of the colony. A honey bee flies about 15 miles an hour, fast for such a tiny insect.

- The average worker makes about $\frac{1}{12}$ teaspoon of honey in her lifetime. To produce 1 pound of honey might require honey bees to visit five million flowers and include flights totaling more than 100,000 miles.

- A foraging bee visits fifty to one hundred flowers on every collection trip it makes from hive to blossoms.

- Honey bees have the ability to tell their hive mates where to find the best nectar by doing a kind of dance, called a waggle. It's a sophisticated, fascinating, and complex system—think honey bee GPS.

- The youngest workers are kept busy feeding the developing larvae (from eggs laid by the queen) and taking care of the queen's every need.

The Anatomy of a Bee

- The bee's body is a well-designed engine. Bees have five eyes and long tongues to reach deep into blossoms to suck out the nectar. The nectar is stored in a pouch, or honey stomach, where enzymes begin the process of breaking down its sugars.

- Next, consider their furry bodies and six legs. As the bees visit the flowers for nectar, flower pollen attaches to their hairs. Seemingly accidental, Mother Nature's design is necessary for pollen distribution, or pollination, essential to much of our agriculture.

- The bees groom the collected pollen into "pollen baskets" or small pouches on their hind legs. Pollen is composed mostly of protein that is an essential nutrient for a bee's survival.

- Each bee has four strong wings that flap constantly, creating the buzzing noise we hear. These wings serve bees well on the many miles they travel as they collect nectar and pollen.

- Inside the hive, the flapping wings evaporate the water content of the nectar, which prevents the honey from fermenting.

- Bee wings flap nearly 25,000 times a minute. No wonder they die of exhaustion.

- Glands in the abdomens of adult worker bees excrete secretions that form the waxy hexagons that become honeycomb, which is used to store the honey and hold the larvae for future honey bees.

- Glands in the heads of young workers secrete royal jelly, which is fed to all larvae, some that will then develop into a replacement queen. She will step up when the existing queen is driven away by the younger queen, the hive gets too crowded, or she retires.

- Bees are relatively passive insects and use their stingers only when defending the hive. The stinger is attached to the bee's abdomen. It embeds in its victim, and when the bee flies away its abdomen tears, causing it to die.

"Beekeeping is farming for intellectuals."
—Sue Hubbell, *A Book of Bees . . . And How to Keep Them*

The Role of the Beekeeper

- Beekeeping is an art of antiquity. Beekeepers also are called apiarists, and anapiary is a collection of hives or colonies of bees.

- Early beekeepers kept colonies of bees in coiled straw hives or skep (to this day the symbol of beekeeping), clay pots, plain wooden boxes, or hollowed-out logs.

- The problem with these early hives was that the beekeeper had to destroy the bee colony to harvest the honey.

- By 1851, L. L. Langstroth designed a box with movable frames that allowed the honey to be removed without destroying the colony.

- Improved versions of the original Langstroth design give the beekeeper the freedom to slide out the frames to inspect the honeycombs and check on the health of the hive.

- To harvest the honey, the frames slide into a large cylindrical tube called a centrifuge. It is turned by human or electronic energy, and from the centrifugal force the honey flows from the honeycomb attached to the frame.

- The box-frame hive influenced many other improvements for more efficient hive management and transformed the industry.

- The U.S. Department of Agriculture estimates there are between 139,600 and 212,000 beekeepers in the United States.

- In recent years backyard beekeeping (usually with fewer than twenty-five hives) has grown in popularity. Some hobbyists have expanded to develop small industries producing artisanal honey.

- For single-origin honey, beekeepers must be diligent in monitoring the activities in their hives, moving them near the blossoms of choice. Over the winter, when most bees are dormant, beekeepers transfer the hives to a safe place and carefully tend them to keep the hives and the bees healthy and thriving.

- During the seasons when pollination is essential for the production of crops, some beekeepers will transport hundreds of hives thousands of miles so the bees can pollinate particular types of blossoms.

- Commercial honey producers move their hives to allow the bees to produce copious amounts of honey and simultaneously pollinate crops.

- In 2010 the U.S. honey crop was valued at $281.9 million, according to the Department of Agriculture.

- Colony collapse disorder is the mysterious dying-off of bee colonies in record numbers. Since the disorder was first reported in 2006, intensive research has focused on finding the causes. The problem is potentially devastating not only because it threatens to destroy the livelihood of many beekeepers but also because bees are the major source of pollination for about ninety crop plants, fruits, and vegetables, including almonds, clover, oranges, apples, cherries, cranberries, blueberries, and canola.

honey and terroir

Terroir, a French word meaning soil, is commonly used when discussing the flavor profile of wine grapes. Today we hear it used in a broader context to describe flavor variations in products such as rice, celery, tomatoes, and honey. When it comes to the specifics of honey, *terroir* refers to the environmental conditions producing the nectar in a particular flower or mixture of flowers. These conditions are hours of sunshine, rainfall, temperature fluctuations, and a host of other variables that ultimately will determine when flowers bloom and, more important, the quality of the nectar's sweetness, fragrance, and overall composition. Therefore, it is safe to say that *terroir* is just as important as the intuitive practices of individual beekeepers in determining the unique character of each and every jar of honey.

"To make a prairie it takes a clover and one bee,
One clover, and a bee,
And revery.
The revery alone will do,
If bees are few."

—Emily Dickinson

The Colors of Honey

The floral sources—or particular blossoms—of the nectar influences the color, fragrance, thickness, texture, and flavor of the honey. Honey is found in an array of colors including almost white, pale yellow, golden, light amber, dark amber, and brown. Lighter-colored honeys generally have a milder flavor but with a pronounced floral aroma often accompanied by herbal, spice, vanilla, butterscotch, or other enticing flavor notes. As the honey gets darker in color, the aroma and taste become more distinctive. This is when such words as "robust," "assertive," and "big" are used as descriptors.

Types of Honey

Honey is available in six basic forms:

- Liquid honey is the most popular. It is most convenient as a table honey and as an all-purpose honey used in cooking and baking. It is extracted from the honeycomb by spinning in a centrifuge or by relying on gravity to drain it from a honeycomb-filled frame in a box-style bee hive. It can be pasteurized (heated to delay crystallization) or left in its raw state. Raw honey can be minimally heated or strained to remove extraneous matter (bee wings, propolis, or wax, for instance), or it can simply be drained from the honeycomb. Raw honey contains natural pollen from the blossoms and some trace minerals, and for those and other reasons it is preferred by many.

- Comb honey is still in its original hexagonally shaped wax "containers" produced with wax that has been excreted by bees. It is cut into chunks and sold in packages. The wax is edible (but not digestible).

- Chunk-style honey or cut comb honey are chunks of honeycomb suspended in a jar of liquid honey. It is one of my favorites. I spoon it on yogurt or ice cream.

- Crystallized or granulated honey is high in glucose, which causes the honey to crystallize quickly. Most honey will crystallize over time. The honey is still perfectly good and is preferred by many as a table honey. If your honey has crystallized and you prefer a liquid honey, set the jar in a metal bowl or pan of water that has been heated to about 130°F and let it stand until the honey is liquefied. It also can be very gently heated in a microwave on low power for 5 to 10 seconds (never longer), depending on the quantity. Heating honey in a microwave is a last resort as it destroys any beneficial minerals, pollen, and flavor notes, so make sure it is warmed only enough to liquefy.

- Creamed or whipped honey is honey that has been processed in its crystallized state so that at room temperature it will maintain its easily spreadable crystallized state. It is a favorite for spreading on bread.

- Flavored or infused honey is usually a mild-tasting honey that is flavored with interesting ingredients. I have tasted several available commercially, and among my favorites are honey infused with cocoa nibs; fresh rosemary, lavender, mint, and other herbs; fresh ginger; vanilla bean; and cinnamon sticks. But there are many others. (See Toasted Walnuts in Honey and Toasted Marcona Almonds in Rosemary Honey in Quick Hits: Sweets, page 177.)

THE ADORABLE, UBIQUITOUS HONEY BEAR

"Isn't it funny
How a bear likes honey?
Buzz! Buzz! Buzz!
I wonder why he does?"
—*Winnie-the-Pooh* by A. A. Milne

Most honey is sold in a wide-mouthed glass or plastic jar, some with a convenient pouring spout. Perhaps the most nostalgic honey container is the cute and squeezable bear. Wearing a pointy cap with an opening at its tip—the perfect size for dispensing a thick stream of honey—the honey-filled bear is called "poetry in plastic" by Betty Cornfeld and Owen Edwards in their book *Quintessence*. I call it perfection. This lovable bear (circa 1958), chubby paws clasping its belly, was created by Woodrow Miller and Ralph Gamber, of the Miller Honey Company and the Dutch Gold Honey Company in Lancaster, Pennsylvania, and supposedly inspired by Yogi Bear. I wonder whether Pooh, the legendary honey lover introduced to us by A. A. Milne in *Winnie-the-Pooh* three decades earlier, had an impact as well. Today, similar honey bears with the familiar pointy cap in a wide array of colors can be found in supermarkets, natural food stores, and farmers' markets.

honey and healing

- The ancient Romans, Greeks, and Chinese used honey to treat wounds. Hippocrates and Aristotle wrote of its healing powers. In the Koran, honey is said to be a remedy for illnesses.

- Ayruveda medicine, a form of medicine originating in India more than four thousand years ago, teaches that honey is important for maintaining balance in the body and promoting healing.

- One of the many reasons honey is of interest in contemporary medicine is because one of its many components is hydrogen peroxide.

- Honey has a pH of 3.2 to 4.5, which is acidic enough to prevent the growth of some bacteria.

- Some sufferers of seasonal allergies swear that raw honey containing pollen from local blossoms gives relief (although there is no scientific evidence).

- Unlike most honey, manuka honey from New Zealand (see page 27) contains high levels of methylglyoxal, which studies indicate may be the reason for its antibacterial properties. This unique honey is at the center of many clinical studies.

- Clinical studies have shown that manuka honey is a very effective treatment for methicillin-resistant *Staphylococcus aureus* (MRSA) infection.

- Folk remedies involving honey are legendary, and the list is long. Honey is thought to help with sore throats, coughs, intestinal disorders, wound infections, swelling and scarring, eye ailments, hay fever and other allergies, burns, joint pain, heart health, blood pressure (specifically borage honey), and insomnia. Take your pick. Because a spoonful of honey a day can't hurt, and might help, it is a sweet way to take your meds.

- Honey was a popular wound dressing during World Wars I and II before the introduction of antibiotics in the 1940s.

- The antimicrobial properties of propolis, a substance manufactured by bees from resins collected from plants, has been recognized for centuries for its wound-healing powers (see next page).

- Hippocrates recognized the benefits of bee venom therapy for treating joint pain. Today the practice known as bee sting therapy is used to treat arthritis, inflammation, and autoimmune conditions.

What Is Propolis?

Propolis, often called nature's antiseptic and considered by many to be a superior healer, is a mixture of plant gums or resins collected by the bees from beeswax, bee saliva, and pollen and made into a kind of sticky mixture. It is used by the bees to repair cracks in the hive to protect and insulate it from inclement weather. This reddish brown substance also reinforces the honeycomb so it can hold the weight of the honey. It makes the hive antibacterial and antimicrobial, rendering it a sterile environment.

Before the discovery of antibiotics, propolis taken directly from the hive was known as an effective healer for serious wounds. The hives, filled with bees making honey, were taken into battle by early medics for a healing remedy and by cooks for sustenance. Today we don't have to carry around a beehive to scrape propolis for our personal use but can purchase it in health stores in the form of ointment, cream, capsule, or resin.

tasting and cooking with honey

the taste of honey: a guide to honey varieties

Fortunately, bees make plenty of honey to feed their own community and us humans, too. When we absorb the magic and complexity of what bees must do to make honey, it is not too farfetched to consider bees and their honey a gift from the universe. The National Honey Board reports at least three hundred varieties of honey in the United States. Worldwide there are probably as many as three thousand types of honey. Keep in mind that no two honeys are exactly alike. Think of wine terms like *terroir* and *microclimate*, which are only two variables that affect what's blooming, the properties in the flower nectars, and where the bees will find their food.

The following list of honeys is only a small representation of what is out there. The purpose of the list is to present an educated estimation of what that nectar in a jar will taste like when you get the jar home and open it. And because this is a cookbook on pairing honey and food, each entry lists simple suggestions for using the honey.

The list consists primarily of single-origin or monofloral honey, which means that by carefully attending the hives, moving them closest to where a specific flower is blooming, and watching where the bees are foraging, the beekeeper can ascertain as closely as possible the origin of at least 50% of the honey. Two exceptions are wildflower and clover honeys, which for reasons of logistics are from multiple sources.

Acacia

Acacia honey is from blossoms of the black locust tree or false acacia. (There also is honey called black locust.) The tree, more like a shrub, is native to eastern North America but is planted from Greece, where it is revered, to the Himalayas.

COLOR: Light gold to almost white but sometimes darker

TEXTURE: Smooth and runny

TASTE: Delicately sweet with soft floral notes

USES: Enjoy this honey simply spread on toasted bread or drizzled on ricotta, cottage cheese, or thick yogurt. Use it to sweeten batter for baked goods and as a tea sweetener. It is excellent paired with a salty young Pecorino Romano, feta, or other aged sheep's milk cheese.

Alfalfa

The bees love the purple blooms on summer alfalfa. It grows profusely from the Midwest to the far West and parts of the Northeast United States, where it is an important crop for feeding livestock.

COLOR: Light yellow to light amber

TEXTURE: Moderately thick

TASTE: Mild to less sweet than other honeys, with distinctive but soft spice notes

USES: An excellent table honey, it is popular along with orange blossom and clover honey for everyday use. It works well as a sweetener in baked goods and for adding sweetness to savory recipes.

Apple Blossom

The sweet nectar from apple blossoms, which bloom in the spring, is collected by honey bees across North America and the United Kingdom.

COLOR: Dark amber

TEXTURE: Thick

TASTE: Rich, bold, and assertive; mildly sweet with soft bitter notes

USES: Spread this luscious table honey on buttered whole-grain toast. Its big flavors pair well with rich, fatty cheeses such as Cheddar, aged Gruyère, Gorgonzola dolce, and aged sheep's milk cheese.

Avocado

Busy bees suck the nectar from avocado tree blossoms while collecting pollen. The trees depend on bees for pollination.

COLOR: Dark amber

TEXTURE: Smooth, rich, and very thick

TASTE: Robust with deep caramel flavor and molasses-like flavor notes

USES: Avocado honey works well when paired with chocolate and pecans, hazelnuts, or other nuts. It is equally delicious used as a table honey spread on buttered toast or drizzled on pancakes and waffles. Try it over ice cream and topped with toasted salted pistachios.

Bamboo

Bees collect the nectar for U.S. bamboo honey from the blossoms of the Japanese knot-weed plant, which is also known by a host of other names (not a true bamboo, a U.S. bamboo is in the buckwheat family). It is considered an invasive plant but is an excellent nectar source for bees when little else is blooming.

COLOR: Dark amber to brown

TEXTURE: Moderately thick

TASTE: Rich and flavorful with tropical fruit flavor notes

USES: Bamboo honey is a good choice for baking, marinades for grilled food, or barbecue sauces.

Basswood

Bees gulp nectar from the fragrant, cream-colored blossoms on the basswood or linden tree, found throughout the northern United States.

COLOR: Pale yellow to golden

TEXTURE: Moderately thick

TASTE: Green apple spice, distinctive with somewhat woodsy and tangy hay and herbal notes; an acquired taste

USES: Use basswood honey on sautéed pork chops or chicken with caramelized apples, mustard, and herbs. It also is delicious drizzled over baked apples or used to sweeten apple cobbler.

Blackberry

Honey bees provide the pollination necessary for the blackberry industry in California and the northwestern states of Washington and Oregon. In my experience this is the one of the few fruit blossom honeys that have the aroma and flavor of the fruit.

COLOR: Light to dark amber

TEXTURE: Thick and prone to crystallization

TASTE: Mild but rich and sweet with delightful notes of blackberry in both taste and aroma

USES: I like it drizzled on a mélange of fresh fruit, especially if it includes blackberries. Make a blackberry sundae by drizzling blackberry honey over scoops of ice cream and top with fresh berries, or make a blackberry parfait by layering honey with yogurt and fresh blackberries. The honey can be used as a sweetener in blackberry cobbler, pie, or turnovers. Use it to deglaze the pan used to sauté chicken, duck, or pork, or brush it on grilled salmon or chicken and serve with a fresh blackberry salsa or salad.

Blueberry

Honey bees love the sweet nectar from the tiny white blossoms of the blueberry shrub and play an important role in pollinating the crop. Unlike blackberry honey, blueberry honey does not have the distinctive fruit taste.

COLOR: Amber

TEXTURE: Moderately thick, soft, and buttery

TASTE: Toasty, butterscotch notes, herbal finish, reminiscent of lavender

USES: This is an excellent table honey. It is delicious added to fruit salad, as ice cream topping, drizzled on pancakes and waffles, as a sweetener in baked blueberry desserts, or in Honey Butter (page 49).

Buckwheat

Honey bees are drawn to the irresistible fragrance of the profuse white flower clusters of buckwheat plants. Buckwheat is not a grain but a fruit seed (we know it as kasha) related to rhubarb and sorrel. It grows freely worldwide.

COLOR: Dark amber to brown but varies by region

TEXTURE: Thick and rich

TASTE: Malty, robust molasses, spicy, assertive, memorable

USES: Buckwheat honey is the perfect sweetener for gingerbread and other spice-laced baked goods. It is a great glaze for sweet potatoes and winter squash. It makes a delicious and distinctive-tasting topping for pancakes and waffles. Buckwheat honey is popular among contemporary mead (see page 151) producers.

Chestnut

Nectar from the sweet chestnut tree, common in Europe, gives us chestnut honey. Italian and Spanish chestnut honey is readily available in specialty food shops in the United States. A blight destroyed U.S. chestnut trees a century ago, making domestic chestnut honey rare.

COLOR: Dark amber to very dark brown

TEXTURE: Thick and viscous

TASTE: Slightly bitter and not overly sweet. It has a pungent herbal aroma and high content of tannin, mineral salts, and pollen. Chestnut honey is considered by some to be an acquired taste.

USES: Chestnut honey is memorable with certain cheeses, especially ricotta, Pecorino Romano, and Gorgonzola dolce, accompanied by sweet pear slices and toasted walnuts. Toss a dish of chestnut-stuffed ravioli with warm chestnut honey, butter, and grated Parmigiano-Reggiano. Swirl chestnut honey into bowls of steaming pureed chestnut soup.

Clover

Probably the most popular—and most popularly priced—honey, clover honey is found in pantries worldwide. Of more than two hundred species of clover, fewer than ten contribute to honey production. Clover is grown primarily as food for livestock. Much of the clover honey on the market is polyfloral, meaning it isn't purely from clover blossoms. However, this does not detract from its luscious sweet honey taste.

COLOR: Light golden to amber

TEXTURE: Mildly thick; tends to crystallize

TASTE: Sweet, delicate floral aroma and taste, with a lasting sweetness on the palate

USES: Clover honey is widely used as a table honey, as a sweetener for tea and coffee, and in baked goods, salad dressings (great in coleslaw and Honey Mustard Salad Dressing, page 114), custards, and sauces.

Cotton Honey

Once again bees are important pollinators, this time for the cotton industry. And bees make copious amounts of honey from cotton flowers. Cotton is in the mallow family and is related to hollyhocks, hibiscus, and okra, so it's no wonder the honey is so delicious.

COLOR: Light in color

TEXTURE: Soft, buttery, and thick. Because of its high sugar content, it crystallizes quickly. It is often creamed (see page 12).

TASTE: Distinctive floral notes with a pleasant tang

USES: In the South, cotton honey is a favorite all-purpose table honey used in baking and as an everyday sweetener. It is used to sweeten beverages such as lemonade and tea.

Cranberry

During the blooming season, which can be as short as two weeks, beehives are set in the bogs in cranberry-growing regions throughout the North to help pollinate the plants. Cranberry honey is a bonus.

COLOR: Medium amber with a pale red cast when a jar of honey is held up to light

TEXTURE: Moderately viscous

TASTE: A luscious, rich, and complex honey, it has a distinctive cranberry taste without the tartness of the raw berry.

USES: Brush cranberry honey on roasted turkey breast or other poultry. Use it to make Honey Butter (page 49) and slather on cranberry bread or muffins. It will sweeten and reinforce the cranberry flavor in Cranberry, Apple, and Ginger-Honey Relish (page 111) or to sweeten your favorite cranberry sauce. It adds an extra flavor dimension to chocolate sauce or chocolate pudding.

Eucalyptus

Eucalyptus is native to Australia but is grown prolifically in California. There are many species of eucalyptus, and flavors vary. One called Blue Gum is from Australia. A much-prized eucalyptus honey comes from Sardinia. The mentholated aroma and taste of eucalyptus make it a popular health remedy, but it is also widely used in savory dishes and in baking.

COLOR: Light to medium dark amber

TEXTURE: Thick and rich

TASTE: Cool, minty taste, menthol flavor notes, complex herbal notes linger on palate

USES: For a more complex flavor hit, eucalyptus makes an excellent table honey. Try it on toast, muffins, pancakes, or ice cream. It is also good brushed on grilled foods such as eggplant and sweet potatoes or spooned over fried bread dough or corn fritters.

Fireweed

Fireweed is a tall perennial plant with bright red-purple flowers. It grows throughout western Canada and the Northwest United States (including Alaska), where it blooms from July through September. It is the only major source of honey that grows so far north.

COLOR: Light in color

TEXTURE: Moderately runny

TASTE: Delicate, mild fruit, grassy, and sweet

USES: Enjoy it drizzled on sliced oranges, in fruit salads, and stirred into lemonade or other fruit drinks. Fireweed honey is best when paired with other mild or delicately flavored foods.

Goldenrod

Goldenrod covers meadows, fields, pastures, and roadsides throughout North America. Its long blooming season—midsummer until the first frost—provides plenty of nectar for the bees.

COLOR: Golden, like the color of the flower

TEXTURE: Thick, viscous, crystallizes quickly

TASTE: Sweet and spicy, with a bit of a bite at the finish. The aroma can be pungent and off-putting at first but mellows with every bite and when used in baking.

USES: Goldenrod honey is a good choice as an all-purpose table honey. It works well in baking.

Heather

Heather honey, from the blossoms of Ling Heather, is rare. It is from true heather found on the moors of Scotland, England, and Ireland, and to a lesser degree in Germany. Heather honey (also called summer or autumn heather) is unique. Because of its gel-like consistency, the bees are unable to evaporate its moisture. Too thick for spin extraction, the honey must be pressed from the combs. It's a popular honey to buy by the comb.

COLOR: Dark amber and slightly cloudy

TEXTURE: Very thick, gel-like

TASTE: Assertive floral, woody, herbal, tangy, slightly bitter, smoky

USES: The Scottish liquor Drambuie is made from malt whisky, heather honey, herbs, and spices. It is also an essential ingredient in Atholl Brose, an unusual drink made with oatmeal, and is popular as a sweetener in holiday eggnog. Melt this thick honey in hot tea or warm custard and pudding, or stir with mustard and curry and use as a basting sauce on game or poultry. It is historically noted for its medicinal properties.

Leatherwood

Leatherwood trees have large white blossoms that yield copious amounts of nectar. The trees grow in the pristine northern wilderness of Tasmania, an island off the southeast coast of Australia and the location of a World Heritage Site.

COLOR: Light to dark amber

TEXTURE: Smooth, thick, viscous, creamy; tends to crystallize

TASTE: Musky and spicy, robust with a complex lingering taste; mildly sweet

USES: To enjoy leatherwood honey's complex flavor notes, drizzle it on ice cream, spread it on buttered toast, and enjoy it with big-flavored cheeses such as Stilton, Bleu d'Auvergne, aged Gouda, or Gruyère.

Lehua

To produce this delicate honey, bees gulp nectar from the beautiful red flowers that grow on the 'ohi'a lehua tree, an indigenous Hawaiian species.

COLOR: Pale gold

TEXTURE: Smooth and silky; tends to crystallize

TASTE: Sweet, delicate floral taste with strong butterscotch notes

USES: Popular as an all-purpose table honey, especially in its native Hawaii, where it is the preferred sweetener for tea.

Lemon Blossom

Blossoms of the lemon tree have long, delicate pinkish-white petals bursting with nectar. Most lemon blossom honey comes from Europe. Among my favorites is a Sicilian type.

COLOR: Light gold

TEXTURE: Smooth; tends to crystallize

TASTE: Bright, fresh taste with a citrus, rather than specifically lemon, taste

USES: This is lovely drizzled on fresh ricotta or sliced strawberries enhanced with shreds of lemon zest. Use to make Honey Butter (page 49) with added lemon zest, and spread on lemon muffins, currant scones, or lemon bread. Stir equal parts of lemon blossom honey with fresh lemon juice and brush on grilled fish. Drizzle the honey on crostini or crackers and spread with fresh goat cheese. The combination is reminiscent of lemon meringue pie.

Macadamia

This is a rich honey made from the fragrant white blossoms of the Hawaiian macadamia nut tree, which is actually native to Australia.

COLOR: Opaque amber

TEXTURE: Soft and very thick

TASTE: Bold, rich taste; caramel and butterscotch notes with a tangy tropical fruit finish

USES: This distinctive honey is delicious with chocolate, especially when accented with macadamia or other nuts as in cake, brownies, and cookies. Drizzle it on pancakes, fritters, or toast.

Manuka

From the blossoms of the manuka or tea tree of New Zealand and Australia, this unique honey is distinguished by its scientifically proven antibacterial properties. In Australia, the honey is known as tea tree honey (not related to tea tree oil). The plant is more of a bush than a tree.

COLOR: Dark tan or amber

TEXTURE: Creamy gel-like consistency (which makes it difficult to harvest); tends to crystallize but melts immediately on the tongue

TASTE: Rich and not overly sweet; herbal, maltlike, earthy flavor notes; slight menthol taste

USES: Delicious eaten with a spoon (the way I like it). Its thick consistency makes it a good choice to spread on crackers, toast, or bread.

Mesquite

Grown in the American Southwest, mesquite trees are valued for their hardwood. Bees love the nectar that flows from mesquite tree blossoms.

COLOR: Dark amber or brown

TEXTURE: Viscous like molasses; crystallizes

TASTE: Haunting smoky aroma (like the wood) and taste

USES: Its smokiness makes it a natural for barbecue sauces and basting grilled meat and vegetables. Because the flavor stands up to soy or tamari, it is a good choice for stir-fried dishes.

Orange Blossom

Orange trees in bloom are a leading source of nectar for honey bees. Orange blossom honey is available worldwide. It is often from a mix of citrus blossoms. Because it is readily available and reasonably priced, it is a staple in many kitchens.

COLOR: Light to medium dark

TEXTURE: Moderately thick

TASTE: Sweet with mild floral and perfumelike notes

USES: This is an all-purpose table honey that is good in baking, salad dressings, marinades, vegetable dishes, or any recipe made with fresh fruit and vanilla.

Palmetto

Honey bees pollinate the tall, beautiful palmetto trees found along the Southeast coast from North Carolina to Florida.

COLOR: Light amber

TEXTURE: Runny

TASTE: Robust, woodsy, herbal notes

USES: It is excellent drizzled on melon slices, tossed with fresh berries, and poured over pancakes. Its full-bodied taste goes well with buttery, fat, and salty cheeses such as provolone, Dubliner, or Pecorino Romano.

Pine

Pine, fir, or forest honey is a unique product made from honeydew, sweet juices excreted by sap-sucking insects, usually aphids and scale insects. Bees collect honeydew as they would nectar. Pine honey sometimes is called honeydew honey. It is produced throughout Europe, New Zealand, Australia, and, in a limited quantity, in Northern California. Its antibacterial properties are said to equal or surpass manuka honey.

COLOR: Amber to dark brown

TEXTURE: Viscous, not prone to crystallization

TASTE: Complex, robust, mineral, concentrated herb and methal notes; reminiscent of dried figs.

USES: The savory flavor notes in this honey make it perfect for salad dressings, marinades made with rosemary or thyme, basting chicken or fish, and pairing with cheese.

Pumpkin Blossom

The blooms on pumpkin blossoms produce enough nectar to keep bees in a pumpkin patch and human honey consumers well fed. Pumpkin blossom honey is found throughout the United States wherever pumpkins are grown.

COLOR: Amber

TEXTURE: Viscous

TASTE: Complex flavor with high spice notes

USES: Use this robust honey in all of your pumpkin recipes, from soup to muffins. Excellent drizzled on Cheddar cheese or pancakes, or used to sweeten whipped cream for gingerbread or spice cake. Use it to make Walnut and Honey Sauce (page 177).

Raspberry

While pollinating raspberries, honey bees take the nectar from the blooms and produce a delicious honey.

COLOR: Light amber

TEXTURE: Viscous and smooth

TASTE: Pleasantly sweet with subtle floral flavor notes and a slight raspberry essence finish

USES: Drizzle raspberry honey on a mélange of berries, melon, peaches, and pears. Puree raspberries, sweeten with raspberry honey, and serve over ice cream, panna cotta, or vanilla custards, or use the honey to spike a glass of sparkling wine or seltzer water.

Rewarewa

Bees produce an excellent honey from the blossoms of New Zealand's rewarewa tree. Although bees enjoy the nectar produced by the blossoms, in this rare instance it is birds that pollinate the plant. The honey produced from rewarewa has antibacterial and antimicrobial benefits often compared to those of manuka honey.

COLOR: Light amber with a reddish-brown tint

TEXTURE: Viscous and soft

TASTE: Dark caramel taste, smoky, spicy flavor notes, intriguing maltlike taste

USE: Use this complex-tasting honey as an ingredient in barbecue sauce, as a glaze for grilled foods, or on sweet potatoes and winter squash. It is delicious spooned over ice cream or frozen yogurt.

Rosemary

The nectar from tiny sky blue flowers of the rosemary plant makes a beautiful honey reminiscent of the taste of the herb. Rosemary grows prolifically in a Mediterranean climate, which is why most of the rosemary honey in our markets is from Italy, France, and Spain.

COLOR: Amber

TEXTURE: Viscous

TASTE: Mildly sweet and fragrant with soft floral notes and herbal minty finish (rosemary belongs to the mint family).

USES: Enjoy rosemary honey drizzled over a round of fresh goat cheese or brush it on pear, peach, or fig halves and broil until golden and topped with snipped fresh rosemary. It makes an excellent glaze for roasted chicken, pan-seared pork chops, or broiled lamb steaks. Rosemary honey is a classic served with salty blue-veined cheese such as Oregon blue, Roquefort, or Stilton. For a special treat use it to make Walnut and Honey Sauce (page 177).

Sage

Sage honey is available only when adequate rainfall has enabled sage blossoms to bloom. Among the many species of sage, Black Button Sage (sometimes called Black Sage) makes an especially lovely honey. It is mostly available in the Northwest.

COLOR: Light amber

TEXTURE: Smooth, moderately thick, tends not to crystallize

TASTE: Mixture of distinctive yet delicate herbal notes; mild and not overly sweet

USES: Sweeten your favorite cornbread with a few spoonfuls of sage honey and then spread or drizzle the results with Honey Butter (page 49) enhanced with minced fresh sage. It is delicious drizzled over slabs of grilled or roasted eggplant and sweet potatoes or tossed with a mixture of roasting vegetables including carrots, turnips, and onions. Add sage honey to a cheeseboard along with aged Gouda or Manchego.

Saguaro

Saguaro honey is from the native cactus of the Sonoran Desert of Arizona and California.

COLOR: Amber, depending on regional source

TEXTURE: Viscous, tends to crystallize

TASTE: Distinctive with spice and vanilla notes

USES: Enjoy saguaro honey as a topping for vanilla ice cream, corn pancakes, or fritters. It is also used as a glaze for roasted, grilled, or pan-seared meats or added to a recipe for barbecue sauce.

Snowberry

Although snowberries are unpalatable to humans, honey bees love the nectar from their blossoms. Snowberries grow in the Northwest, primarily Oregon and Idaho.

COLOR: Amber

TEXTURE: Soft and lovely as it melts on the palate

TASTE: Delicate sweet butterscotch and fruity flavor notes

USES: Enjoy snowberry honey drizzled on ice cream, pancakes, and waffles, and stirred into Greek yogurt.

Sourwood

Sourwood honey is revered by Southerners and honey connoisseurs. The sourwood tree grows in the Appalachian and Blue Ridge Mountains from southern Pennsylvania to North Georgia. Producing it is a challenge for even the most expert beekeeper because of scarce numbers of sourwood trees, the importance of sunlight and rain to ensure ample nectar, and short bloom times (June–August). Blossoms hang in drooping clusters of tiny bell-shaped flowers that resemble lily of the valley. The honey is considered a rare treat.

COLOR: Ranges from very light yellow to pale amber

TEXTURE: Smooth and buttery

TASTE: Light and sweet with spicy and floral notes with hints of cinnamon, allspice, ginger, and anise

USES: To savor sourwood honey's flavor notes, spread it on buttered toast and corn muffins, or drizzle it on pancakes and corn fritters. It also can be used to baste grilled chicken or pork tenderloin or as an ingredient in barbecue sauce. Use it to make Honey Butter (page 49).

Star Thistle

Farmers consider star thistle a noxious weed, but bees love it and the honey is gorgeous.

COLOR: Golden

TEXTURE: Runny with a tendency to crystallize over time

TASTE: Mildly floral, minty, herbal, vanilla notes, pleasant tang

USES: Star thistle is a great table honey. Use it on toast and muffins and stirred into tea. It is enjoyed when used to sweeten sliced strawberries or peaches, drizzled on ice cream or yogurt, mixed with peanut or almond butter to make a sandwich spread, and used in fruit sorbets or to sweeten tea.

Sunflower

Worldwide, fields of sunflowers are the perfect source of nectar for foraging honey bees.

COLOR: Pale yellow

TEXTURE: Typically runny; tends to crystallize

TASTE: Minty with a touch of menthol and a bit of a tang

USES: Use sunflower honey as an all-purpose table honey, for baking, as a tea sweetener, and as a glaze for roasted vegetables and meats.

Thyme

The mountainsides throughout Greece and Sicily are covered with wild thyme. The honey produced from the nectar of thyme blossoms has been revered since antiquity and is often mentioned in ancient poetry.

COLOR: Dark golden to amber

TEXTURE: Thick and rich, sometimes creamed

TASTE: Lively, complex herbal quality; robust flavor with mint notes; toasty

USES: Drizzle on Pecorino Romano, feta, or other sharp, salty, fatty cheese. Excellent on eggplant fritters or grilled or roasted eggplant slices. Use it as a spread on toast or crackers.

Tupelo

Tupelo trees grow in the wetlands of Florida and Georgia, where for only a short time their round, spiky blossoms drip with nectar so sweet it inspires song lyrics: "sweet as tupelo honey, just like honey from a bee." Beekeepers elevate the hives to keep them out of the water and tend the hives by boat. Truly a labor of love, tupelo is sometimes called swamp honey.

COLOR: Golden to light amber; opaque

TEXTURE: Runny without crystallization

TASTE: Floral notes in both aroma and on the palate; buttery notes and bright, sweet, clean finish

USES: Tupelo honey is the preferred table honey in regions where it is harvested. It is used as a spread for toast, hot muffins, and popovers; a sweetener for hot cereal; and a topping on ice cream and pudding.

Wildflower

Wildflower is a polyfloral honey made from the nectars from a wide variety of blooms that change with the seasons and regions. Samples of the honey differ greatly, depending on where it is produced, but of all the samples I've tasted they all have some of the following characteristics. It is one of my favorite all-purpose honeys.

COLOR: Shades of amber from light to dark, depending on the season

TEXTURE: Thick and smooth, sometimes crystallizes or is creamed

TASTE: Complex with all sorts of flavor notes from anise to mint to green apple

USES: Wildflower honey is a great all-purpose table honey to use for baking and in almost all recipes where a complex touch of sweetness is needed.

Wild Oak

A rare honey from the flowers of the wild oak trees that grow in a rich agricultural area called Lleida, located southwest of Barcelona, Spain.

COLOR: Dark brown

TEXTURE: Smooth and thick

TASTE: Complex, rich, molasses with caramel notes

USES: This is a beautiful honey to serve with a salty, rich, blue-veined cheese such as a Cabrales from Spain, but it also will work with Stilton and a Point Reyes or other domestic blue cheese. It can be enjoyed poured over vanilla ice cream or rice pudding. Use it to sweeten custard or panna cotta. For a satisfying but simple treat, tear off a chunk of warm baguette and drizzle with this superb honey.

guidelines for a honey tasting

A honey tasting is fun, but don't select too many or you'll suffer palate fatigue. Three to five varieties are doable. Here are some guidelines to get you started.

- Provide a list of the honeys to be tasted, giving some background information such as origin and where it was purchased.

- The categories under each honey should be color, texture, taste, and uses.

- Provide pencils so that tasters can document their impressions of each honey being tasted.

- Think wine tasting, but don't challenge yourself by tasting the honey blind (without the names to identify them) unless you are an experienced honey taster.

- Like wine, honey should be tasted from the lightest in color to the darkest because generally color indicates the flavor notes. Light honey is mild and soft tasting, and dark honey is generally more complex and assertive.

- Before tasting, observe the color and aroma of the honey.

- To avoid wasting any precious honey I prefer to taste directly from the jar. Provide plenty of small plastic spoons that can be discarded or washed between uses. Metal espresso spoons can be used, but you need to have plenty on hand to discourage double dipping, and in some cases the metal can alter the pure taste of the honey.

- Provide water and plain crackers or baguette slices and thin slices of apple for freshening palates between tastes.

- Have fun sharing impressions and comparing notes along the way.

- Taste is subjective, and we all have different sensory capabilities. Someone might taste vanilla, while another person will taste citrus.

- Encourage creativity by coming up with a variety of descriptors. Some typical words used to describe honey are soft, floral or flowery, buttery, caramel, spice, herbal, vanilla, cinnamon, astringent, tannic, woodsy, molasses, rich, malty, licorice, toasty, grassy, menthol, and of course sweet. (You'll experience some honeys that taste sweeter than others.)

- Talk about the foods, spices, or seasonings you imagine paired with a particular honey. Possibilities include apples, chocolate, pork ribs, walnuts, ginger, Cheddar cheese, vanilla ice cream, and mustard.

Honey and Cheese Tasting

Seated around a conference table laden with jars of honey and platters of cheese, Juliana Uruburu and I had a deliciously tough task ahead of us. Juliana, the cheese buyer for Market Hall Foods in Oakland, California, and The Pasta Shop in Berkeley, had selected cheeses and honeys from her stores, and I had brought along honey from my extensive home collection. Between us we had assembled more than a dozen honeys to taste with as many cheeses. We were excited to do the deed.

Juliana, a knowledgeable and passionate cheese expert, pre- pared a tasting sheet listing the cheeses from the mildest to the strongest in flavor. Much like tasting wine, we moved from the soft, mild tastes of the honey and the cheeses to the bigger, bolder-tasting samples. Generally, light-colored honeys have distinctive sweet, floral, and sometimes herbal notes, and as the hue of the honey darkens the flavors become more complex with, for example, tannic, toasty, butterscotch, molasses, or chocolate flavor notes.

We began by sniffing the honey to detect any distinctive aromas and then took a tiny taste on the tip of a spoon. We noted the flavor sensations. We then spooned a small pool of honey on a thin slice or cube of cheese and tasted. These are the questions we asked ourselves: Do we like it? Does the combination sing on our palate and in our mouth? The most successful pairings occurred when neither the honey nor the cheese was dominant. Instead we looked for the two to be in harmony as new and exciting flavors popped on our palates. An indication of an excellent pairing was when we kept going back for more.

Here are some of our favorite honey and cheese combinations:

Sicilian orange blossom honey with Burrata (creamy, fresh mozzarella-type cow's milk cheese) or a cow's or sheep's milk ricotta

Sicilian lemon blossom honey with Rove des Garrigues (tangy, slightly acidic fresh goat's milk cheese) or other type of fresh goat cheese, Burrata, or ricotta

Lavender honey with Burrata or ricotta

Wildflower honey with Brillat-Savarin (semisoft triple crème, bloomy rind cow's milk cheese), Époisses (semisoft stinky washed rind cow's milk cheese), Cheshire (aged Cheddar-style cheese), or Point Reyes blue (salty and aged raw blue cow's milk cheese)

Pine honey with a smoked blue cow's milk cheese from Oregon (Rouge Creamery) or Wisconsin (Moody Blue), or an aged Cheddar-style cheese

Thyme blossom honey with Coupole (semisoft goat cheese), Rove des Garrigues or other type of fresh goat cheese, or a creamy cow's milk feta

Eucalyptus honey with Rove des Garrigues or other type of fresh goat cheese, Brillat-Savarin, Petit Basque (semihard cheese from Pyrenees sheep's milk), or Parmigiano-Reggiano (hard raw cow's milk cheese)

Sunflower honey with Brillat-Savarin, Coupole, or Éspoisses

Chestnut honey with Petit Basque, Beemster X.O. (hard, aged cow's milk Gouda)

Leatherwood honey with Benning (semihard goat's milk Gouda), Roth Käse Moody Blue (delicately smoked cow's milk from Wisconsin), Rogue Creamery Smokey Blue (delicately smoked cow's milk from Oregon), or an aged Cheddar-type cheese

Honeycomb with Camembert (creamy cow's milk), Brie, Stilton, or other salty, creamy, blue-veined cheese

cooking with honey

Primitive people considered honey found in its natural state to be a heavenly gift worth the bee stings suffered as they took honey from the hive. But as the primary sweetener—sugar wasn't discovered until much later—honey was used in sweet and savory dishes from the time people first began to document the art of cooking.

Apicius, a famous Roman gastronome from whom we get the word "epicure," created many recipes with honey, including a classic sauce for fish (see page 80 for my grandmother's version). In *History of Food* by Maguelonne Toussaint-Samat, the author describes a delicious-sounding dish of milk combined with fermented honey to create soft curds, which sounds like an early version of honey cheese. Toussaint-Samat also mentions an early American dish of beans with honey and says the early Algonquins of Canada cooked small pumpkins stuffed with honey in burning embers. From earliest times, honey was used to make sauces for meats and poultry, as a poaching liquid for stuffed fig leaves and fruits, for soaking pastries (think baklava), and for preserving fruit and meat (think honey cured turkey or ham).

In contemporary kitchens honey is popular used as a sweetener for tea, spread on buttered toast, or drizzled on hot cereal. When honey is plentiful it is often used in place of sugar for baked goods. But because prolonged heating will erase the subtle flavor nuances in many varietal honeys, it is recommended that the cook stick with light-colored, mild-tasting, and economical honey such as alfalfa, orange blossom, or clover for a neutrally sweet honey taste in recipes for Honey-Orange Muffins (page 43) or Honey Oatmeal Raisin Cookies (page 139). For a bold caramelized taste, use dark amber buckwheat, apple, or other big-flavored fruit blossom honey or wildflower honey in recipes for Apple, Pecan, and Honey Spice Cake (page 152) and Chunky Peanut Butter and Honey Cookies (page 144). For an unusual honey-sweetened tasting experience, a bold-tasting dark amber honey— mesquite, eucalyptus, avocado, or buckwheat—is a revelation when paired with the chocolate in Micki's Special Honey Fudge Brownies (page 148) or Velvety Honey-Chocolate Pudding (page 173).

Honey, because of its unique composition, behaves differently when used for baking. Follow the simple guidelines in Baking with Honey (page 137) to ensure the success of the recipes.

Save your precious varietal honeys with delicate floral notes for recipes that require a minimum of heat or no heat at all. Fireweed honey is outstanding in Honey Zabaglione (page 169) lavender honey is sublime in Honey Panna Cotta (page 171) lemon blossom honey is perfect for the Honey Ricotta Pudding (page 174), and tupelo honey is excellent in Orange, Mango, and Ginger Sorbet (page 163). Feel free to experiment on your own, swapping out your own favorites for the varietals suggested in the recipes.

When it comes to savory recipes, there is more to the art of cooking with honey than the power of its sweetness. To be pleasing to the palate, a dish needs to have a balanced flavor profile. Think sweetness, salt, acid, fat, and heat congregating in your mouth so that the message to your brain is, "Please give me more". To taste good, a dish requires at least three of these components distributed in a harmonious manner so that no one taste dominates.

Obvious ingredients that help to balance the flavor profile when honey is used for sweetness are lemon juice or vinegar for acid; minced jalapeño, a dash of hot sauce, grated ginger, or curry powder for spice; and soy or tamari for salt. Two examples of this flavor-balancing act are—acidic cranberries, sweet apple, spice, and heat of ginger, and, of course, the honey—in the recipe for Cranberry, Apple, and Ginger-Honey Relish (page 111) and—the acid of rice vinegar, the salt of soy sauce, the heat of red pepper—in the recipe for Crispy Coconut Shrimp with Tangy Honey Dipping Sauce (page 77).

To complete the equation, fat in the form of butter, olive oil, cheese, or bacon and other meats is essential for satiety and to carry the other flavors. The recipe for Pear, Stilton, and Bacon Salad with Honey-Glazed Pecans (page 117) is a perfect example of how the sweetness of the honey is the thread that connects the flavors of the salty cheese, fatty bacon, and acid of the red wine vinegar. This connective harmony among the sweetness of the honey, acidity of the vinegar and the tomatoes, and the salt of the preserved lemons, is evident in the recipe for Moroccan-style Stewed Tomatoes and Fennel with Honey and Preserved Lemon (page 128).

The choice of which varietal honey to use in a savory recipe depends on the flavor profile of the recipe. For the Crispy Fish Fillets in Sweet and Sour Sauce (page 80), a honey with the gumption to stand up to the acid and salt notes in the sauce is best. Not a bold-tasting buckwheat, but a moderately assertive honey with some interesting flavor notes of its own such as an oregano, thyme, or star thistle honey would work. Whereas for the Salmon with Honey, Miso, and Ginger Glaze (page 79) a mild-tasting orange blossom or clover honey that will soften the punch of the miso, rice vinegar, and ginger without masking their unique flavors is best. At the other end of the spectrum, the best honey to use in the Sweet and Sour Meatballs (page 90) laced with fiery hot Sriracha, a healthy portion of cider vinegar, and a touch of cinnamon is a big bold buckwheat, dark wildflower, or spicy apple blossom.

Each of the following recipes suggests a type of honey to use, but none of the suggestions are etched in stone. Let your own taste be the final judge.

The bottom line when cooking with honey in either sweet or savory recipes is to taste as you cook—both the recipe and the honey choices—and ultimately balance the sweetness to your own liking. The good news is that the range of tastes of honey is endless and cooking with honey knows few limits.

breakfast
and snacks

"The King was in his counting house
Counting out his money;
The queen was in the parlour
Eating bread and honey"

—An eighteenth-century
Mother Goose nursery rhyme

{ TYPE of
HONEY }

I've made these with light floral honey such as orange blossom, acacia, or tupelo but also like to use a more assertive honey such as an amber wildflower or buckwheat. Experiment and then double the heady honey taste by using the same variety in the Honey Butter recipe.

honey-orange muffins

Makes 12 muffins

These moist muffins are irresistibly crunchy, not from nuts but from tiny beads of millet. Serve them with Honey Butter (page 49) or Orange Honey Butter (page 49) and watch them vanish.

1½ cups unbleached all-purpose flour

1 cup whole wheat flour

¼ cup uncooked millet

1 tablespoon finely chopped orange zest

1 teaspoon baking powder, sifted

1 teaspoon baking soda, sifted

1 teaspoon ground cinnamon

½ teaspoon coarse salt

2 large eggs, at room temperature

1 cup plain nonfat or low-fat yogurt

½ cup honey

½ cup unsalted butter, melted

1. Preheat the oven to 350°F. Lightly coat the muffin tin with butter or nonstick cooking spray.

2. Place the all-purpose flour, whole wheat flour, millet, orange zest, baking powder, baking soda, cinnamon, and salt in a large bowl and stir to combine.

3. In a small bowl, whisk the eggs, yogurt, honey, and butter until well blended.

4. Add the liquid ingredients to the dry ingredients and stir until well blended. The batter will be very thick.

5. Divide the batter evenly among the muffin cups. Bake for 18 to 20 minutes, until the tops are golden and a toothpick inserted in the center of a muffin comes out clean. Let cool slightly on a wire rack before removing from the pan. These are delicious warm from the oven and smeared with Honey Butter (page 49), or can be wrapped in aluminum foil and reheated or split and toasted.

With a few exceptions the different flavor notes among varieties get lost when honey is baked in a batter, so I generally use a light-colored mild clover or orange blossom honey in most baking recipes. But if you have a favorite wildflower or alfalfa honey on hand, it would be delicious in these tender muffins.

honey double corn muffins

Makes 12 to 16 muffins

Here is a savory muffin made with cornmeal and corn kernels—fresh off the cob, if in season. Serve for breakfast or brunch or with a steaming bowl of soup for lunch. For a fun variation, fold a cup of fresh blueberries into the batter just before baking.

1½ cups all-purpose flour

1 cup coarse cornmeal

2 teaspoons baking powder, sifted

½ teaspoon baking soda, sifted

1 teaspoon coarse salt

1 cup corn (frozen and thawed, canned and drained, or fresh kernels), blotted dry between paper towels

2 large eggs

1 cup buttermilk

6 tablespoons unsalted butter, melted

⅓ cup honey

1. Preheat the oven to 400°F. Lightly coat the muffin tin with butter or nonstick cooking spray.

2. Place the flour, cornmeal, baking powder, baking soda, and salt in a large bowl and stir to combine. Add the corn and stir to coat with the dry ingredients.

3. In a separate bowl, whisk the eggs, buttermilk, melted butter, and honey until well blended. Add to the dry ingredients and gently combine using a rubber spatula.

4. Divide the batter evenly among the muffin cups. Bake for 20 to 25 minutes, until the tops are golden and a toothpick inserted in the center of a muffin comes out clean. Let cool on a wire rack before removing from the pan. Serve with Honey Butter (page 49) or, for a savory hit, Chipotle Honey Butter (page 49).

{ TYPE OF HONEY } *Use all-purpose table honey. Orange blossom and clover are both reliably good in baking.*

honey, scallion, and cheddar scones

Makes 12 scones

The secret to making flaky, tender scones is to handle the dough as gently and as little as possible. The dough is supposed to be sticky, so resist the temptation to add more flour. These are delicious served warm, especially when slathered with Honey Butter (page 49).

3½ cups all-purpose flour

2 tablespoons baking powder, sifted

½ teaspoon coarse salt

6 tablespoons cold unsalted butter, cut into small pieces

1 cup plus ½ cup coarsely shredded sharp Cheddar cheese

⅓ cup thinly sliced scallions (white and green parts)

1 cup half-and-half

⅓ cup plus 2 tablespoons honey

2 large eggs, beaten

1. Preheat the oven to 400°F. Spray two baking sheets with nonstick cooking spray.

2. Place the flour, baking powder, and salt in the bowl of a food processor and pulse to blend. Add the butter a few pieces at a time and pulse until the mixture resembles coarse crumbs. Transfer to a large bowl. Add 1 cup of the cheese and the scallions and toss to blend.

3. In a small bowl, whisk the half-and-half, ⅓ cup of the honey, and eggs until thoroughly blended. Slowly add to the dry ingredients, tossing with a fork after each addition. Toss just until the mixture is evenly moist. Do not overmix.

4. Using a rubber spatula, gather the sticky dough and turn out onto a well-floured work surface. With floured hands, separate the dough into 12 even portions and pat into 2½-inch-wide rounds. Place 1½ inches apart on the baking sheets.

continued on page 46

5. Warm the remaining 2 tablespoons of honey in a microwave for 5 seconds or in a small saucepan over low heat until thinned. Brush the honey on the top of each scone and sprinkle evenly with the remaining ½ cup of cheese.

6. Bake for 20 to 25 minutes, until dark golden brown. Let cool on the baking sheets for 10 minutes. Serve warm or at room temperature. These are best eaten the day they are baked, but they also freeze well.

Because of the natural presence of clostridium bacterial spores, honey should not be fed to children under the age of one year.

So that the corn flavor comes through loud and clear I prefer a mildly flavored, sweet all-purpose honey such as orange blossom or clover. But you might want to try wildflower, sourwood, basswood, or alfalfa.

honey cornbread with earl's honey butter sauce

Makes 8 to 12 servings

The benchmark for this recipe was a delicately crumbed sweet cornbread I enjoyed at the Honey House Café in Port Costa, California. Earl Flewellen, the beekeeper and co-proprietor of the Honey House Café, serves warm wedges of cornbread and traditional pound cake covered with his caramelized Honey Butter Sauce. (See more about Earl and his sauce recipe on page 158.) To give the cornbread a savory hit, substitute Chipotle or Sriracha Honey Butter (page 49) or drizzle a slice with wildflower, leatherwood, or eucalyptus honey and top with a sliver of aged Cheddar, Gruyère, or Comté cheese. Make the slivers or curls of cheese with a vegetable peeler or a cheese plane. I love this served with Honey-Glazed Bacon (page 55).

1 cup fine yellow cornmeal	1 cup buttermilk
¾ cup all-purpose flour	6 tablespoons unsalted butter, melted
2½ teaspoons baking powder, sifted	¼ cup honey
½ teaspoon baking soda, sifted	1 large egg
½ teaspoon coarse salt	Earl's Honey Butter Sauce (page 158)

1. Preheat the oven to 400°F. Lightly butter an 8- or 9-inch round or square baking pan.

2. Place the cornmeal, flour, baking powder, baking soda, and salt in a large bowl and stir until blended.

3. In a separate bowl, whisk the buttermilk, butter, honey, and egg until well blended. Add to the flour mixture all at once and stir with a rubber spatula until well blended. Pour into the pan and spread in an even layer.

4. Bake for 18 to 20 minutes, until the edges are golden and a toothpick inserted in the center comes out clean. Let cool on a wire rack. Serve warm or at room temperature with the honey butter sauce.

In most baked goods I use everyday orange blossom or clover honey, but for a more distinctive taste I sometimes use a full-flavored, darkly hued buckwheat honey or a distinctively floral, rich, amber-colored wildflower honey.

banana, honey, and pecan bread

Makes 1 loaf

Being a banana bread aficionado, I couldn't resist including this quick bread. Bananas sliced into a bowl of yogurt and drizzled with honey are a favorite breakfast treat, so I thought, why not combine the bananas and honey in a basic banana bread recipe? The all-purpose and whole wheat flours complement the pecans, contributing to the all-around rich, moist, and nutty taste of the bread.

½ cup (1 stick) unsalted butter, softened

½ cup lightly packed light brown sugar

½ cup honey

2 large eggs, at room temperature

1 cup mashed ripe bananas (about 2 large bananas)

1 teaspoon vanilla extract

1 cup unbleached all-purpose flour

1 cup whole wheat flour

1 teaspoon ground cinnamon

1 teaspoon baking powder, sifted

½ teaspoon baking soda, sifted

½ teaspoon coarse salt

½ cup chopped pecans

1. Preheat the oven to 325°F. Lightly coat a 9 by 5 by 3-inch loaf pan with butter or non-stick cooking spray.

2. Place the butter and brown sugar in the large bowl of a stand mixer and beat until light and fluffy. Gradually beat in the honey in a slow, steady stream. Add the eggs, one at a time, beating well after each addition. On the lowest speed, blend in the bananas and vanilla.

3. In a separate bowl, combine the flours, cinnamon, baking powder, baking soda, and salt. On low speed, gradually add the dry ingredients to the butter mixture until blended. Fold in the pecans with a rubber spatula.

4. Scrape the batter into the loaf pan and smooth it on the surface and into the corners of the pan. Bake for about 45 minutes, or until the top is browned and the edges pull away from the sides. Let cool thoroughly on a wire rack. Run a small metal spatula around the edges and turn out onto a plate or cutting board.

This is the place where your most flavorful varietal honey will shine. Some of my favorites are made with avocado honey, fireweed honey, safflower, and tupelo honey, to name only a few.

honey butter

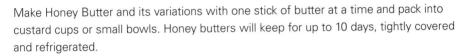

Makes ½ to ¾ cup

Make Honey Butter and its variations with one stick of butter at a time and pack into custard cups or small bowls. Honey butters will keep for up to 10 days, tightly covered and refrigerated.

½ cup (1 stick) unsalted or salted butter, softened

¼ cup honey of choice

Place the butter and honey in a small bowl and blend with the back of a fork until combined. Pack into a custard cup or small bowl and refrigerate, covered tightly, until ready to use. Soften to room temperature for easy spreading.

Variations:

CINNAMON HONEY BUTTER: Add ½ teaspoon of cinnamon or a spice of choice to Honey Butter and blend. Taste and adjust accordingly. Spread on muffins, quick bread, or toast, or melt on pancakes or French toast.

ORANGE HONEY BUTTER: Use orange blossom or lemon blossom honey. Add 2 teaspoons of finely chopped orange rind (orange part only, if possible), or 1 teaspoon of finely grated orange zest. Use on grilled endive or romaine hearts cut in half, cooked asparagus, popovers, warm muffins, toast, pancakes, or French toast.

STILTON HONEY BUTTER: Use clover or other mild honey, wildflower, or buckwheat. Add 1½ ounces of crumbled Stilton cheese and stir to blend. Use on steamed asparagus or broccoli, roasted cauliflower steaks, whole wheat crostini, baked potatoes, or grilled steak.

SRIRACHA HONEY BUTTER: Use clover or other mild honey, wildflower, or buckwheat. Add 2 teaspoons of Sriracha, or more to taste. Stir into polenta, grits, or mashed potatoes, or melt on grilled swordfish.

CHIPOTLE HONEY BUTTER: Use clover or other mild honey, wildflower, or buckwheat. Add 1½ teaspoons of finely chopped chipotles in adobo sauce, or more to taste. Stir into cornmeal grits, spread on corn muffins or cornbread, melt on grilled salmon, or spread under the skin of chicken breasts before roasting or grilling.

HERB HONEY BUTTER: Use herb honey such as sage, thyme, oregano, or rosemary. Add 2 teaspoons of finely chopped fresh herb leaves such as sage, thyme, oregano, or rosemary. This is excellent on cooked vegetables, breads, and grilled meats or seafood.

Once honey is caramelized it is difficult to pick out the subtle nuances that are present in uncooked honey, so for this recipe I stick with a mild table variety such as clover, alfalfa, or orange blossom.

honey french toast

Makes 4 servings

Thick slices of rustic bread, soaked with a mixture of milk, honey, eggs, and vanilla, brown quickly in a pool of hot butter. Honey is drizzled over the golden, eggy slices and allowed to quickly caramelize in the hot skillet. Serve plain, with Earl's Honey Butter Sauce (page 158), or with a summery mixture of sliced peaches macerated in honey, lime juice, and snipped mint.

6 thick (¾-inch) slices white or whole-grain bread cut from an oval rustic loaf

1 cup milk

2 large eggs

2 tablespoons honey

1 teaspoon vanilla extract

Ground cinnamon, to taste (optional)

1 to 2 tablespoons unsalted butter

⅓ cup honey, or more to taste

Earl's Honey Butter Sauce (page 158) or Peaches with Honey and Mint (page 53)

1. Place the bread in a single layer in a large, shallow roasting pan or baking dish.

2. In a bowl, whisk the milk, eggs, honey, and vanilla. Pour evenly over the bread. Soak for about 30 minutes, tilting the pan often and using a spoon to distribute the milk mixture over the bread. Press the bread lightly with the back of the spoon to encourage it to absorb all of the liquid. Sprinkle with the cinnamon.

3. Heat a heavy skillet large enough to hold the bread in a single layer, over medium heat. Add the butter and tilt the pan until the butter melts and evenly coats the bottom. Add the soaked bread and cook for about 3 minutes, or until browned on the bottom, adjusting the heat to maintain a steady but gentle sizzle. Turn the bread with a wide spatula and brown the other side for about 3 minutes. Drizzle the honey evenly over the tops and cook for about 1 minute, or until the honey begins to bubble. Turn the bread over and brown the other side, spooning the bubbling honey over the top.

4. Transfer the French toast to a platter and serve plain, with warmed honey butter sauce, or topped with Peaches with Honey and Mint (page 53).

Use any mildly sweet honey with floral or fruity notes such as acacia; clover; orange, lemon, blackberry, raspberry blossom, or tupelo.

peaches with honey and mint

Makes 4 servings

Use this sauce as a topping for yogurt, ice cream, pound cake, Sweet Cheese Tart (page 153), Honey Panna Cotta (page 171), or Honey French Toast (page 50). This simple sauce also can be made with nectarines, strawberries, or a combination of fresh fruit.

3 to 4 medium-size peaches	1 to 2 tablespoons fresh lime juice
3 tablespoons honey	1 tablespoon torn fresh mint leaves

1. Peel the peaches by placing in a saucepan half-filled with boiling water for about 1 minute, or until the skins are loosened. Transfer the peaches to a bowl of ice water and slip off the skins with a paring knife. Halve and pit the peaches, then cut into thin slices.

2. Gently combine the peach slices, honey, lime juice, and mint. Taste and add more lime juice, if needed, to balance the flavors.

Rather than going bold, I like to use a mild-flavored honey, perhaps an orange blossom, tupelo, star thistle, or clover.

dried sour cherry honey sauce

Makes 4 to 6 servings

Unsweetened dried sour cherries have a wonderfully intense cherry taste. Reconstituted with water (with an optional addition of brandy) and sweetened with a bit of honey, the cherries make a luxurious sauce perfect for French toast, pancakes, pound cake, Honey Panna Cotta (page 171), or Sweet Cheese Tart (page 153). If you can find only sweetened dried sour cherries, decrease the amount of honey by half.

½ cup unsweetened dried sour cherries   1½ cups water

¼ cup brandy (optional)   ¼ cup honey

1. Combine the cherries and brandy in a small bowl and let stand for 30 minutes. If not using the brandy, skip this step.

2. Combine the cherries, brandy, and water in a small saucepan and simmer covered over medium-low heat, for 10 minutes. Remove from the heat, cover, and let stand for about 30 minutes, or until the cherries are plump and soft.

3. Add the honey and simmer the cherries over medium-low heat, stirring often. Cook for 5 to 10 minutes, until the liquid is thickened. Let cool to room temperature and serve.

I like the big flavors in a dark or amber honey, such as avocado, buckwheat, or mesquite, with the taste of bacon.

honey-glazed bacon

This is for those who love the sweetness and chewiness of caramelized honey with their bacon. The combination is quite addictive, even for the uninitiated. I like to serve this sweet version of bacon (I think of it as candied bacon) with French toast or warm cornbread smothered in warmed honey or Earl's Honey Butter Sauce (page 158).

8 bacon slices

4 tablespoons honey

1. Place the bacon in a large, heavy skillet and cook over medium heat until lightly browned but still soft and pliable. Drain on a paper towel. Pour off the fat and wipe the skillet dry.

2. Put the bacon back in the skillet and drizzle with the honey. Cook over medium-low to medium heat until the honey is boiling, turning the bacon until it is coated and caramelized. Transfer the bacon to a plate or a piece of aluminum foil (the bacon will stick to paper towels). As the bacon cools it will become chewy like a caramel candy.

feta cheese and honey omelet

Makes 1 serving

Honey in my Sunday morning cheese omelet was a spontaneous reaction when I eyed a jar of crystallized star thistle honey (see more about crystallized honey on page 12) on the kitchen counter. I knew putting crystallized honey into the omelet would be less messy than using liquid honey. The crystals of honey melted gently in the warmth of the cooked egg and cheese. The result was a delicious omelet with just the right balance from the mild tang of sheep's milk feta and the sweetness and distinctive herbaceous flavor notes in pale yellow star thistle honey. Look for a mild, creamy feta (I love Israeli feta), but I also have made this omelet successfully with crumbled goat cheese.

2 large eggs	2 teaspoons crystallized honey
3 tablespoons cold, crumbled mild feta or goat cheese	Olive oil or butter, for pan

1. Crack the eggs into a small bowl and whisk until well blended. Have the cheese and honey measured and ready.

2. Heat a small heavy skillet over medium heat until hot enough for a drop of water to sizzle. Add a drop of olive oil or a sliver of butter and tilt the pan to cover the surface.

3. Pour the eggs into the pan. The pan should be hot enough to sizzle and start setting the eggs immediately. Decrease the heat to medium-low. Pull the eggs away from the edges of the pan and tilt the pan so that uncooked eggs in the center run to the edges.

4. Sprinkle a layer of the cheese over half of the circle of partially cooked egg. Top with the crystallized honey. Using a small rubber spatula, fold the half of the omelet without the filling over the filled half. Cook on low for about 30 seconds, or until the eggs are set.

5. Slide the omelet onto a plate and serve.

I prefer a mildly sweet, floral orange blossom, alfalfa, or clover honey. But this is also the place to use a honey infused with ginger, lavender, or cinnamon.

popover pancake with honey spiced apples

Makes 4 servings

Sometimes called Dutch Baby Pancake, this easy dish is baked in a skillet. Cast iron is preferred, but any heavy skillet with an ovenproof handle will work. The pancake will puff up dramatically around the edges, resulting in a pool in the center perfect for the apple slices poached in spiced honey. Other fruits can be used. Try it with peaches, nectarines, or pears. Serve this as a brunch dish or dessert.

Pancake	Honey Spiced Apples
3 large eggs	2 or 3 large apples, preferably Golden Delicious
¾ cup milk	
1 tablespoon honey	1 tablespoon unsalted butter
¾ cup unbleached all-purpose flour	½ teaspoon ground cardamom, ginger, or cinnamon
2 tablespoons unsalted butter, cut into small pieces	½ cup honey
	1 tablespoon fresh lemon juice

1. To make the pancake, preheat the oven to 400°F. Place in the oven an 8- or 10-inch cast-iron skillet or heavy skillet with a heatproof handle.

2. Put the eggs, milk, and honey in a large bowl and whisk. Add the flour and whisk until well blended.

3. Using a pot holder, remove the skillet from the oven and add the butter. Tilt the skillet to melt the butter and coat the skillet evenly. Add the batter all at once and return the skillet to the oven. Bake for 18 to 20 minutes, until the pancake puffs up around the edges and is golden brown.

4. While the pancake is baking, make the honey spiced apples. Quarter, core, and peel the apples and cut into ¼-inch-thick wedges. Melt the butter in a medium skillet. Add the apples and cook, stirring gently with a rubber spatula, for about 5 minutes, or until lightly browned on both sides. Sprinkle with the spice of choice. Add the honey and stir to coat the apples. Heat until the honey boils, then add the lemon juice and remove from the heat.

5. To serve, slide the pancake onto a platter. Spoon the apples and honey syrup into the center and cut into wedges, distributing the fruit evenly.

Bees are the only insects that produce and store food in a form that can be used by humans.

{ TYPE OF HONEY }

I like to use a favorite wildflower honey with notes of fennel, thyme honey (Greek thyme honey is amazing), star thistle, or lavender honey in this simple recipe, but any fragrant, full-flavored variety will work.

goat cheese spread with lemon and honey

Makes about 1 cup (8 or more servings)

A log of fresh goat cheese, a bit tangy for some palates, is transformed into a smooth, creamy spread when blended with a bit of lemon zest and a generous drizzle of honey. Show off your most flavorful honey—thyme, oregano, and sage honey are all pretty special—in this delicious spread. The honey is blended into the cheese and then drizzled on top, so you get to savor its taste in every bite. Match the fresh or dried herb garnish to the honey: Use fresh thyme or sage with corresponding honeys, and dried lavender or herbes de Provence with lavender honey.

1 (8-ounce) log fresh goat cheese

4 tablespoons honey

3 tablespoons plain low-fat Greek yogurt

2 tablespoons extra-virgin olive oil

1 small clove garlic, grated

1 teaspoon grated lemon zest (use Meyer lemon if available)

¼ teaspoon freshly ground black pepper

¼ teaspoon coarse salt

1 teaspoon fresh thyme, oregano, sage, lavender, or other herb that matches the herb in the honey (optional)

1. Place the goat cheese in the bowl of a food processor and add 2 tablespoons of the honey, the yogurt, olive oil, garlic, ½ teaspoon of the lemon zest, ⅛ teaspoon of the black pepper, and the salt. Pulse until creamy and well blended. Transfer to a small, shallow serving bowl and smooth the top with a rubber spatula.

2. Sprinkle the spread with the remaining ½ teaspoon of lemon zest and ⅛ teaspoon of black pepper. Drizzle with the remaining 2 tablespoons of honey and sprinkle with the fresh herb.

3. Serve with crackers or crostini as a nibble with drinks or a cup of tea.

I like to use a dark honey with big dried-fruit flavor notes such as buckwheat, wildflower, or leatherwood.

cream cheese, date, and honey spread

Makes about 1 cup (4 to 8 servings)

This unlikely combination is utterly luscious and nostalgic, perhaps because it reminds me of the cream cheese on date and nut bread sandwiches of my youth. The honey is my addition. Spread it on toast or crackers or stuff into celery boats. You can use toasted or untoasted almonds. I am partial to the taste of toasted almonds, so I toast 2 or 3 cups of natural almonds with the skin on in a 350°F oven for 10 to 15 minutes and store them for later use. Otherwise it seems silly to toast a small amount like ¼ cup.

1 (8-ounce) package cream cheese, softened

2 tablespoons honey

¼ cup pitted dates, cut into ¼-inch dice

¼ cup toasted natural almonds (skin on)

1. Place the cream cheese and honey in a small bowl and beat with a wooden spoon until well blended and fluffy.

2. Add the dates and almonds and gently stir to blend. Keep the spread refrigerated and soften at room temperature before using.

A rich, bold, thick amber-hued honey is perfect with the assertiveness of the Stilton. Try one of these: wildflower, wild oak, avocado, apple or pumpkin blossom, leatherwood, or buckwheat.

open-faced honey toast with warmed stilton

Makes 2 to 4 servings

Salty, tangy, blue-veined Stilton cheese is the perfect foil for a rich-tasting honey. This sandwich was inspired by a favorite after-school snack of mozzarella cheese layered on thick-sliced Italian bread and melted under the broiler. These open-faced sandwiches need no embellishment or accompaniment, unless it is a steaming bowl of tomato soup.

4 thick slices (½- to ¾-inch) whole-grain rustic Italian loaf

4 ounces Stilton, crumbled

¼ cup honey

1. Position the top oven rack so that it is within 3 inches of the broiler. Heat the broiler on high.

2. Place the bread on a sheet pan. Watching carefully, broil for 1 to 2 minutes, until lightly browned. Remove the pan from the oven and turn the slices over. Broil for 1 to 2 minutes more. Remove from the oven but leave the broiler on.

3. Spread each slice of bread on one side with about 1 tablespoon of honey and return to the pan. Sprinkle the crumbled cheese on top of each, distributing evenly.

4. Place the pan under the broiler and heat for 1 to 2 minutes, just until the cheese begins to melt. Serve at once.

To balance the fat content and creamy richness of the Cheddar, the salt and crunch of the bacon, and the tartness of the pickle, use a bold-tasting buckwheat or leatherwood, a flavorful wildflower or wild oak, buttery avocado, or a tangy pumpkin or pine honey.

grilled dubliner cheese, bacon, dill pickles, and honey sandwich

Makes 4 servings

Slather chewy multi-grain bread with honey and then add sliced Dubliner, a rich and creamy Irish Cheddar, plus crisp bacon and dill slices. The Dubliner melts into the bacon to make an over-the-top grilled cheese embellished with cool, crunchy pickle slices. The pucker in the pickles balances the sweet honey. Experiment with other cheeses such as aged Gouda, Comté, Gruyère or Petit Basque, a semisoft, aged goat cheese from the Pyrenees.

4 slices bacon

8 slices (scant ½-inch-thick) rustic bread, preferably whole wheat

2 tablespoons melted butter

¼ cup honey

6 to 8 ounces Dubliner or other creamy Cheddar cheese, thinly sliced with a cheese plane

8 slices dill deli sandwich pickles, blotted dry

1. Place the bacon in a large cast-iron or heavy-duty nonstick skillet and cook over medium heat, turning, until crisp. Drain on paper towels and cut slices in half. Let the pan cool, discard the bacon fat, and wipe clean.

2. Spread one side of each slice of bread with the melted butter. Place 4 slices, buttered side down, on a work surface. Spread each unbuttered side of the bread slices with about 1 tablespoon of the honey. Top each with a ¼- to ⅓-inch slice of cheese covering the surface, 2 half-slices of bacon, and dill pickles, cut to fit. Top with the remaining bread slices, placing them buttered side up.

3. Heat the skillet over medium heat until a drop of water sizzles upon contact. Add the sandwiches and adjust the heat to medium-low. Place a lid just a bit smaller than the skillet directly on top of the sandwiches. Cook the sandwiches for about 5 minutes, until the

cheese begins to melt and the bottom slice of bread is golden brown. Using a wide spatula and holding the top of the sandwiches in place with fingertips, carefully turn them and brown the other side for about 5 minutes, adjusting the heat as needed to avoid overbrowning.

4. Transfer the sandwiches to a cutting surface. Let cool slightly and cut them in half before serving.

From spring, when the first blossoms appear, until late fall, when most flowers disappear, bees fly from flower to flower, gulping nectar from 50 to 100 flowers per trip.

{ TYPE OF HONEY }

Choose a honey that goes well with the cheese you intend to use. With Manchego, I use a slightly tannic dark thyme or rosemary blossom honey. If you choose a soft, mild cheese such as fresh goat cheese, select a floral varietal such as orange, lemon, or star thistle. With feta cheese, use Greek thyme, eucalyptus, or pine honey. The combinations are endless.

flatbread with melted manchego, rosemary, and honey

Makes 6 flatbreads

Almost every culture has some type of yeast bread with a topping. Call it pizza, flatbread, or naan. This version is made with pizza dough stretched into ovals and brushed liberally with olive oil. Make them in the oven or on a grill. When almost ready, layer overlapping slivers of Manchego or another salty, aged cheese and heat until melted. Then sprinkle with fresh rosemary (thyme or oregano also would work) and drizzle with your favorite varietal honey.

Yellow cornmeal

Pizza Dough (recipe follows), or 2 pounds store-bought fresh or frozen pizza dough, proofed according to package directions

Extra-virgin olive oil

6 ounces Manchego, or another semi-hard cheese with good melting properties, cut into slivers or curls with a cheese plane or vegetable peeler

1 tablespoon chopped fresh rosemary

½ cup honey

1. Sprinkle 2 baking sheets lightly with cornmeal.

2. Prepare Pizza Dough through step 4. Punch the dough down and let it stand for 10 minutes. Divide the dough equally into 6 portions. On a lightly floured surface, flatten each portion with the heel of your hand and gently stretch from the outside edges into an oval 6 to 8 inches long and about 5 inches wide. Brush olive oil liberally onto both sides. Using a long, flat spatula, transfer the ovals of dough to the baking sheets. Cover them with a towel and let them stand for about 30 minutes.

3. Arrange the oven racks in the lower half of the oven. Preheat the oven to 450°F.

4. Bake the flatbreads for about 10 minutes, or until lightly browned on the bottom. Remove the baking sheets from the oven and carefully turn over the flatbreads. Arrange the cheese on the top (the browned sides) and return the sheet pans, reversing the placement, to the oven and bake for about 5 minutes, or until the cheese is melted.

continued on page 68

5. Sprinkle the melted cheese with the rosemary. Serve the flatbreads warm with about 1 tablespoon of honey, or to taste, drizzled on each.

pizza dough

1¼ cups water, warm (105° to 115°F)

2 teaspoons active dry yeast

1 teaspoon honey

2 tablespoons extra-virgin olive oil

2 teaspoons coarse salt

3½ to 4 cups unbleached all-purpose flour, or more as needed

1. Combine ¼ cup of the warm water with the yeast and honey in a large bowl; stir to blend. Cover the mixture with plastic wrap and let it stand for about 10 minutes, or until foamy.

2. Mix in the remaining 1 cup of water, olive oil, salt, and 1½ cups of the flour, and stir until smooth. Gradually add the remaining 2 to 2½ cups of flour, stirring until the dough comes away from the side of the bowl.

3. Turn the dough out onto a floured surface and knead by hand for about 10 minutes, or until it is smooth and elastic, adding as much extra flour as needed to keep the dough from being too sticky. Alternatively, knead the dough with a dough hook in a stand mixer for about 5 minutes. The dough is adequately kneaded with it springs back when poked with a finger.

4. Shape the dough into a ball and place in a large, oiled bowl. Turn the dough to coat with the oil. Cover the bowl with plastic wrap and let the dough rise in a warm place for about 1 hour, or until doubled in bulk.

5. Punch down the dough and divide and shape as directed in the recipe. If not using the dough right away, punch it down, cover lightly with plastic wrap, and refrigerate for up to 24 hours.

Any honey will shine in this simple drink. Use your favorite.

hot honey lemon tea

Makes 1 serving

This soul-satisfying hot drink is especially comforting when one has a case of the sniffles. But I enjoy it anytime I need a little pick-me-up. If using less acidic Meyer lemons, use less honey. With more acidic lemons such as Eureka, start with a smaller amount of honey and adjust to taste. To make a hot toddy, add a shot of rum, bourbon, or brandy.

1¼ cups boiling water

Juice of 1 lemon (2 to 3 tablespoons)

2 to 4 tablespoons honey, or more to taste

Combine the water, lemon juice, and honey in a large mug. Stir until the honey is dissolved. The recipe can be multiplied to fill a teapot and for multiple cups of tea.

Use your favorite varietal, but if lavender blossoms are available to sprinkle in the pitcher you might want to use lavender honey.

iced honey lemon tea

Makes 4 servings

This is a refreshing treat on a warm summer day. Taste it with each addition of lemon and honey to make sure it is lemony and sweet enough for your taste. Thin slices of lemon and a sprig of mint or lemon verbena add a festive touch.

1 quart cold water

¾ cup fresh lemon juice

4 to 6 tablespoons honey

2 cups ice cubes

1 lemon, seeded and sliced thinly (optional)

Fresh sprigs lavender or a handful of lemon verbena or mint leaves, torn into pieces (optional)

Combine the water, lemon juice, and honey in a large pitcher and stir to dissolve the honey. Add the ice cubes and stir to combine. Taste and add more lemon or honey, if needed. Add the lemon slices and lavender, lemon verbena, or mint.

In this recipe I use whatever honey I have on hand, but I prefer varieties with a slight spiciness to bring out the spice in the apricots, such as star thistle, some wildflower varieties, safflower, goldenrod, or an especially fragrant orange blossom.

honey, banana, and dried apricot smoothie

Makes 1 large serving or 2 smaller servings

If you can find those delicious, dark orange Blenheim apricots, this is the place to use them. They are moist enough to be used straight from the bag. If Blenheims are not available, other dried apricots can be used. Just make sure they are soft and moist. If not, soak them in boiling water to cover for about 30 minutes before using. You can use about 2 tablespoons of the remaining soaking water as part of the liquid in the smoothie.

8 ice cubes

1 cup plain low-fat yogurt

1 ripe banana

⅓ cup (about 2 ounces) moist dried apricots, preferably Blenheim

3 to 4 tablespoons honey

In a blender, combine the ice cubes, yogurt, banana, apricots, and honey. Blend on high speed for 1 minute, pulsing every 2 seconds. Continue blending until the mixture is smooth. Taste and add more honey if you like.

Quick Hits: Breakfast and Snacks

- Spread crystallized or creamed honey on plain crackers, or drizzle liquid honey on warm crostini and top with a cheese such as crumbled feta, Stilton, or Gorgonzola, or a curl of Pecorino Romano or Parmigiano-Reggiano. Star thistle honey is a favorite because it becomes crystallized very quickly and has a distinctive taste that will stand up to the cheese.

- A favorite Catalan dish, *mel i mato*, is a young, soft goat cheese or sheep's milk cheese mounded in a small gratin dish, drizzled with honey, and roasted in a hot oven for a few minutes, or until warmed. Spread on bread and eat with toasted walnuts.

- Mash 2 tablespoons of honey with 4 ounces of softened goat cheese until blended. Spread on a toasted baguette.

- Lemon or orange blossom honey is great with fresh goat cheese. Layer the cheese with arugula leaves and prosciutto slices to make a closed or open-faced sandwich.

- Drizzle a thick, rich sunflower, avocado, or tupelo honey on plain or flavored nonfat or low-fat yogurt or cottage cheese.

- Drizzle lavender, thyme, or star thistle honey on a medley of sliced watermelon, cantaloupe, and honeydew.

- Stir orange blossom, lemon blossom, or blackberry honey, to taste, into plain yogurt. Fold in coarsely chopped fresh strawberries, blueberries, or raspberries.

- Make a breakfast parfait: layer orange segments, plain yogurt, sour cream or crème fraîche, honey, and toasted sliced natural almonds. Or substitute raspberries, strawberries, peaches, nectarines, or melon for the orange.

- Serve thin wedges of tart apples with a slice of buttery aged Cheddar cheese (Dubliner is a good choice) or a well-aged Comté or Gruyère and a drizzle of blackberry, tupelo, blueberry, or orange blossom honey.

- Serve a ripe, sweet pear, cut into thin wedges, with a salty blue-veined cheese (Roquefort, Gorgonzola, or Stilton) and a side of Toasted Walnuts in Honey (page 177). Or drizzle with chestnut honey and serve toasted walnuts on the side.

- Brush halved fresh figs with avocado, wildflower, or another rich, complex honey, stuff a small chunk of blue-veined cheese or soft goat cheese in the center, drizzle with more honey, and grill or broil until warmed. Or skip the cheese and add a drop of aged balsamic to the honey-glazed grilled figs.

- For crackers, celery boats, or a sandwich spread, combine ½ cup of peanut or almond butter and 2 tablespoons of buckwheat, sunflower, avocado, or alfalfa honey.

- Make a quick dip with 1 cup of plain low-fat yogurt, 1 tablespoon of spicy Dijon mustard, and 1 tablespoon of honey. Serve with raw carrots, peeled broccoli stems sliced diagonally, and apple slices. Adjust the mustard and honey to taste.

- For a sleepy-time remedy, stir 1 tablespoon of honey and 1 tablespoon of rum into a mug of hot milk.

main dishes

{ TYPE OF HONEY }

To stand up to the soy sauce, I used a full-bodied honey. I suggest a dark-hued mesquite, pumpkin, or wildflower.

crispy coconut shrimp with tangy honey dipping sauce

Makes 4 servings

Light and crisp with a coating of flaked coconut and panko, these shrimp should be assembled ahead of time so the coating has about an hour to set before they are fried. The dipping sauce is inspired by the sweet jam and crushed red pepper–laced sauce served often in Vietnamese restaurants. This version is lighter and even more luscious.

Shrimp

1 pound extra-large (20 to 24) shrimp, shelled and deveined, tails on, if possible

3 egg whites

1½ cups panko

¾ cup unsweetened flaked coconut

Dipping Sauce

½ cup honey

2 tablespoons unseasoned Japanese rice vinegar

1 tablespoon soy sauce

½ teaspoon crushed red pepper

Vegetable oil

1. Rinse the shrimp and pat dry. Place the egg whites in a shallow bowl and beat until partially frothy. Combine the panko and coconut on a large plate. Line a tray with parchment paper or waxed paper.

2. Dip a shrimp into the egg whites and allow the excess to drip off. Roll the shrimp in the panko mixture. Dip it a second time in the egg, let any excess drip off, and roll in the panko mixture again, pressing the panko gently into the shrimp to make a thick layer. Place the shrimp on the tray. Repeat the double dipping and coating with the panko mixture with the remaining shrimp. Refrigerate for at least 1 hour before frying.

continued on page 78

3. To make the dipping sauce, whisk the honey, rice vinegar, soy sauce, and red pepper in a bowl until well blended. Adjust the amount of red pepper to taste. Place in a small serving bowl and let stand at room temperature.

4. Line a plate with paper towels. Pour ½ inch of oil into a 10-inch skillet and add a crust of bread. Heat over medium heat until the crust sizzles and turns golden brown. Discard the crust. Put the shrimp in the skillet about 8 at a time. Fry for about 1 minute, turn with tongs, and fry the other side for about 1 minute, or until golden. Transfer to the plate to drain. Cook the remaining shrimp, adjusting the heat between medium and medium-low to maintain even browning.

5. Serve the shrimp with the dipping sauce.

{ TYPE OF HONEY } *To allow the flavors of the miso and ginger to come through, I prefer a mild table honey such as clover or orange blossom in this simple glaze.*

salmon with honey, miso, and ginger glaze

Makes 4 servings

A salmon fillet emerges from under a hot broiler with a golden honey glaze spiked with ginger and miso. The salty tang of the miso and the heat of the ginger balance the sweetness of the honey.

2 tablespoons white miso

2 tablespoons honey

1 tablespoon unseasoned Japanese rice vinegar

1 teaspoon grated fresh ginger

12 ounces center-cut salmon fillet, skinless or skin on

1. Arrange the top oven rack so that it is about 4 inches from the broiler. Heat the broiler on high. Line a rimmed sheet pan with aluminum foil.

2. Place the miso, honey, vinegar, and ginger in a small bowl and stir until well blended. Put the salmon in the center of the pan and spread the top with half of the miso mixture.

3. When the broiler is hot, place the pan in the oven and broil for 5 minutes. Remove the pan and spread the remaining miso mixture on top of the salmon. Broil for 5 to 8 minutes more, until the surface of the salmon is well browned and the fish is cooked to desired doneness.

crispy fish fillets in sweet and sour sauce

Makes 4 servings

Traditionally this Venetian dish is made with a mixture of sugar and vinegar and is called *in saor*. But my version, copied from my grandmother, uses honey in place of the sugar. Typically she fried the fish in the late afternoon and then marinated them in the vinegar and honey mixture. At serving time she garnished the dish with raw onion and a sprinkling of raisins. In deference to the sweetness of the honey, I leave off the raisins and add a few capers for a heightened salt note. The dish is best served at room temperature.

4 sturdy fish fillets (about 6 ounces each) such as rock cod, snapper, or salmon, preferably cut from the tail

Coarse salt and freshly ground black pepper

½ cup all-purpose flour

2 eggs

1 cup fine, dry bread crumbs or crushed panko (see note)

1 cup thinly sliced onion, separated into rings

Sauce

½ cup mild red wine vinegar

¼ cup honey

Pinch of coarse salt

Extra-virgin olive oil

1 tablespoon small capers, rinsed, drained, and blotted dry

1. Sprinkle the fish generously with salt and pepper. Spread the flour on a plate and lightly dredge the fish fillets, shaking off any excess. Discard the flour and place the fillets on a tray. Place the eggs in a shallow soup bowl or pie plate and whisk until well mixed. Put the bread crumbs or panko on the dish used for the flour and spread in a thin layer. Dip the fillets one at a time into the egg and let the excess drip off. Coat the fish with the bread crumbs and set aside on a tray. Repeat with the remaining fish. Refrigerate for about 20 minutes.

2. Place the onion in a bowl, cover with ice and water, and let crisp until ready to use.

3. To make the sauce, whisk the vinegar, honey, and a pinch of salt in a deep bowl until well blended. Set aside.

4. Place ½ inch of oil in a medium to large skillet with sloping sides. Add a small crust of bread. Heat over medium heat until the crust is browned. Discard the crust. Add the fish and cook for 2 to 3 minutes, until the bottoms are well browned. Carefully turn with a long, flexible spatula and cook the other side for about 2 minutes, or until browned. Transfer to a large platter.

5. Drain the onion rings and blot with a paper towel. Spread over the fish. Whisk the sauce one more time and drizzle evenly over the onion and fish. Sprinkle with the capers. Serve warm or at room temperature.

It is estimated that to produce 1 pound of honey for human consumption, a hive needs to produce 8 pounds of honey for its own survival. When harvesting honey, beekeepers always leave behind enough to sustain the hive.

I prefer the distinctive taste of star thistle for this savory and sweet mix of flavors. But any full-bodied honey with distinctive floral flavor notes such as lemon or orange blossom or clover will add sweetness without masking the bite of the ginger or the tang of the lemon in the sauce.

chicken cutlets with honey, lemon, and ginger sauce and ginger-honey walnuts

Makes 4 servings

Honey-glazed walnuts spiked with garlic and ginger are so addictive you might want to double the recipe to have extras on hand for snacking. They are great with these tender cutlets coated with tangy honey, lemon, and ginger sauce. This recipe uses a small amount of chicken broth. Keep small amounts on hand by freezing homemade or store-bought broth in ice cube trays or small plastic freezer containers.

Ginger-Honey Walnuts

2 teaspoons extra-virgin olive oil

½ teaspoon grated ginger

1 small clove garlic, grated

½ cup walnut halves

1 tablespoon honey

½ teaspoon coarse salt

Lemon Chicken

1½ pounds boneless and skinless chicken breasts (see note)

Coarse salt and freshly ground black pepper

½ cup all-purpose flour

4 tablespoons extra-virgin olive oil

1 teaspoon grated ginger

1 clove garlic, grated

¼ cup fresh lemon juice

¼ cup chicken broth

2 tablespoons honey

1 thinly sliced scallion (about 1 tablespoon, green part only)

continued on page 84

1. To make the walnuts, place the oil, ginger, and garlic in a small skillet. Slowly heat over medium-low until the garlic sizzles. Add the walnuts and honey. Cook on medium heat for about 2 to 3 minutes, adjusting the temperature until the honey boils and sticks to the walnuts and the walnuts turn golden. Sprinkle with the salt, adjusting to taste. Transfer to a side dish or a sheet of aluminum foil. Do not put on paper towels because they will stick.

2. With a sharp knife, fillet the chicken breasts through the thickest part to make 8 cutlets. Place them on a large piece of plastic wrap, sprinkle with salt and pepper, cover with a second sheet of plastic wrap, and gently but firmly pound the chicken with a meat pounder or the underside of a small, heavy skillet to make fillets of even thickness of ¼ to ⅓ inch.

3. Spread the flour on a large plate and lightly dredge the cutlets; shake off the excess flour.

4. Heat 3 tablespoons of the olive oil in a large, broad skillet until hot enough to sizzle. Add the cutlets a few at a time and cook for 1 to 2 minutes per side, until lightly browned. As the cutlets are cooked, transfer to a platter and cover with foil to keep warm.

5. Discard the oil in the skillet and let the skillet cool slightly. Add the remaining 1 table-spoon of oil, ginger, and garlic to the skillet. Heat and stir over medium-low heat just until the garlic sizzles. Add the lemon juice, chicken broth, and honey. Heat, stirring to loosen any browned bits in the skillet, for about 3 minutes, or until the mixture boils and thickens. Pour the sauce over the chicken and sprinkle with the walnuts and the scallions.

Note: *If your market sells already pounded chicken cutlets, skip step 2.*

Because the mustard is assertive I like to use a sweet, mild honey, such as orange blossom, clover, or alfalfa. But if you are partial to more complex varietals, use wildflower, leatherwood, eucalyptus, or other honey.

chicken legs with tangy honey mustard glaze

Makes 4 to 6 servings

Make this popular dish with a combination of legs and thighs or entirely with one or the other. Either way they will be lip-smacking, finger-licking good. Sriracha is one type of chili sauce made from red chiles, vinegar, garlic, and other ingredients. It is both hot on the palate and hot in the sense that it is all the rage among contemporary cooks. If it's unavailable, use Tabasco or any other favorite hot sauce. You may want to use a chile-infused honey in this recipe, but proceed with caution as it can be very fiery.

8 chicken legs or thighs, or 4 of each	½ cup honey
Coarse salt and freshly ground black pepper	3 tablespoons Dijon mustard
	1 teaspoon Sriracha or other hot sauce

1. Preheat the oven to 350°F. Line a large, rimmed sheet pan with aluminum foil.

2. Sprinkle the chicken on all sides with the salt and pepper. Arrange on the pan.

3. Place the honey, mustard, and Sriracha in a small saucepan. Heat, stirring, until boiling, for about 1 minute, or until the sauce thickens slightly. Remove from the heat.

4. Brush half of the sauce on the chicken, turning to coat. Bake for 25 minutes. Remove the pan from the oven. Use tongs to turn the chicken. Coat the top sides with the remaining sauce. Return the pan to the oven and roast for 25 minutes, until the chicken is a rich golden brown.

stir-fried honey and tamari chicken thighs with green beans and short-grain rice

Makes 4 servings

This is a simple but pretty stir-fry of honey-glazed chicken thighs with green beans. It is perfect for a quick weeknight dinner. Use cold leftover rice or cook the rice ahead and cool to room temperature before using.

1 pound green beans, stems trimmed and cut in 1-inch lengths

2 tablespoons honey

2 tablespoons tamari or soy sauce

1 tablespoon toasted Asian sesame oil

2 teaspoons grated fresh ginger

1 clove garlic, grated

8 skinless and boneless chicken thighs, fat trimmed, halved

1 tablespoon vegetable oil

3 cups cooked short-grain brown or white rice, cooled

¼ cup thinly sliced scallions (green part only)

1. Heat a saucepan half filled with water to a boil. Add the beans and boil for about 3 minutes, or until crisp-tender. Drain and set aside.

2. Whisk the honey, tamari, sesame oil, ginger, and garlic in a medium-size bowl. Add the chicken and stir to coat.

3. Heat a large skillet or wok until hot enough to sizzle and evaporate a drop of water. Coat the pan with the oil. Add the chicken, reserving the marinade, and cook over medium heat, 2 to 3 minutes, turning with tongs, until the chicken is nicely browned. Adjust the heat as needed so the chicken cooks without getting black.

4. Add the rice, green beans, and reserved marinade. Cook, stirring with a spatula, for about 5 minutes, or until well blended and very hot. Sprinkle with the scallions and serve.

I reach for a bigger, bolder-flavored honey for any dish with tamari or soy sauce. Try avocado, amber wildflower, buckwheat, goldenrod, or apple blossom honey.

honey and orange-glazed chicken thighs with sesame seeds

Makes 4 servings

This extremely quick and easy recipe is made with boneless and skinless chicken thighs. In summer serve it on a bed of greens for a main-dish salad, or for a cool-weather dish serve it on a bed of brown rice.

6 to 8 boneless and skinless chicken thighs, fat trimmed

Coarse salt and freshly ground black pepper

2 tablespoons extra-virgin olive oil

2 cloves garlic, thinly sliced

¼ cup fresh orange juice

2 tablespoons honey

2 tablespoons tamari or light soy sauce

2 teaspoons brown sesame seeds (optional)

1. Rinse the chicken and pat dry with paper towels. Sprinkle both sides with salt and pepper.

2. Heat a large, heavy skillet or a wok over medium heat. Add the olive oil and garlic and cook until the garlic sizzles but does not brown. Add the chicken and cook on one side for about 5 minutes, or until lightly browned, adjusting the heat as needed. Turn the chicken and cook for about 5 minutes, or until lightly browned.

3. Add the orange juice and honey. Bring to a boil and cook for about 3 minutes, turning the chicken until coated and cooked through. Continuing to turn the chicken, add the tamari, and cook over high heat for about 1 minute, or until blended and almost all of the juices are evaporated. Sprinkle with the sesame seeds.

I like a dark honey with a bold taste such as leatherwood, wildflower, wild oak, avocado, or buckwheat.

chicken stewed with tomatoes, green olives, and orange

Makes 4 servings

Inspired by chicken cacciatore, this is a simple stovetop version of browned chicken simmered in tomatoes seasoned with honey and orange zest and topped with green olives. The contrast in flavors—acidic tomatoes, sweet honey, and salty olives—makes the dish especially satisfying. Serve with noodles, rice, or mashed potatoes to soak up the delicious chunky sauce.

2 to 2½ pounds chicken pieces (2 legs, 2 thighs, and 2 breasts, or any combination)

Coarse salt and freshly ground black pepper

½ cup all-purpose flour

3 tablespoons extra-virgin olive oil

½ cup chopped onion

½ cup chopped celery

½ cup chopped carrot

2 cloves garlic, chopped

1 strip (½ by 3 inches) orange zest, julienned or finely chopped

1 teaspoon chopped fresh thyme leaves

½ cup dry white wine

1 (28-ounce) can diced tomatoes with juices

3 tablespoons honey

¼ cup pitted and coarsely chopped brine-cured green olives

1. Sprinkle the chicken with salt and pepper. Place the flour on a plate and lightly dust the chicken, shaking off excess flour.

2. Heat the oil in a large, deep skillet with a lid or a shallow braising pan until hot enough to sizzle a piece of chicken. Place all of the chicken in the skillet, adjusting the heat to keep it sizzling. Cook the chicken, turning, for about 10 minutes, or until it is lightly browned on all sides. Transfer the chicken to a dish. Spoon off all but ½ tablespoon of oil in the skillet.

3. Add the onion, celery, carrot, garlic, orange zest, and thyme to the skillet. Cover and cook over medium-low heat for about 10 minutes, stirring occasionally, until the vegetables are very soft but not browned. Add the wine, increase the heat to high, and boil, uncovered, until the wine is reduced by half.

4. Add the tomatoes. Boil and stir over medium-high heat for about 5 minutes, until the tomato juices are reduced and the sauce is thickened. Stir in the honey. Add the chicken and any juices in the dish to the tomato sauce. Sprinkle with the olives.

5. Cover the skillet and, turning the chicken once or twice, cook on medium-low heat for 15 to 20 minutes, until the chicken is cooked through. Taste the sauce and add salt and pepper, if needed.

{ TYPE OF HONEY } *Use any honey you have on hand, although I find that big-flavored wildflower, buckwheat, or fruit blossom honey will stand up to the big flavors in the tomato sauce.*

sweet and sour meatballs

Makes 4 servings (about 32 meatballs)

This is a contemporary version of the once-popular 1950s cocktail meatballs made with currant jelly and chili sauce. Here the tender, succulent meatballs are spiced with Sriracha, pureed tomatoes, honey, and apple cider vinegar. Serve with toothpicks reminiscent of the chafing-dish version or serve for dinner with rough mashed potatoes and cooked greens or steamed broccoli. There won't be any leftovers.

Meatballs

1 cup soft, fresh bread crumbs

½ cup water

1 large egg

1 pound lean ground beef

¼ cup raisins

1 tablespoon extra-virgin olive oil

½ cup chopped yellow onion

1 clove garlic, grated

1 teaspoon coarse salt

1 teaspoon Sriracha or other hot sauce

½ teaspoon grated fresh ginger

Sauce

1 (28-ounce) can whole or diced tomatoes with juices

¼ cup honey

¼ cup apple cider vinegar

1 teaspoon Sriracha

½ teaspoon ground cinnamon

½ teaspoon coarse salt

1. Place the bread crumbs and water in a large bowl. Let stand for about 5 minutes, or until the bread has absorbed the water. Beat the egg into the mixture with a fork. Crumble the ground beef into the bowl. Add the raisins and set aside. Do not mix yet.

2. In a small skillet, heat the olive oil until hot enough to sizzle a piece of onion. Add the onion and stir over medium heat for about 3 minutes, or until translucent. Add the garlic and cook for about 30 seconds. Add the onion and garlic to the bowl with the ground beef. Add the salt, Sriracha, and ginger. Gently combine the ingredients. Do not squeeze mixture with your hands because it will make the meatballs too compact. Refrigerate the meatball mixture for about 30 minutes.

3. Preheat the oven to 400°F. Spread a sheet pan with a sheet of parchment paper or aluminum foil.

4. Have ready a small bowl of cold water to wet your hands while shaping the meatballs. Pinch off 1-inch pieces of the meatball mixture and roll in wet hands to form balls. The mixture will be moist and soft. Line up the meatballs, about ½ inch apart, on the pan. Bake for 15 to 20 minutes, until browned.

5. While the meatballs are browning, make the sauce. In a food processor fitted with a metal blade, puree the tomatoes, honey, vinegar, Sriracha, cinnamon, and salt. Transfer to a large, deep skillet or Dutch oven and heat to boiling. Boil the sauce over medium heat, stirring occasionally, for about 15 minutes, or until thickened and reduced by half.

6. When the meatballs are browned, use a spatula or slotted spoon to add them to the sauce. Gently spoon the sauce over the meatballs and cook covered on low heat for 5 minutes. Serve in bowls with sauce spooned on top, or serve from a chafing dish on small plates with forks or toothpicks for spearing.

With so many big flavors in this dish, I prefer to use my everyday orange blossom or other neutral honey for the sweetness needed to balance the saltiness of the fish sauce.

vietnamese-style beef stew with star anise, honey, and fish sauce

Makes 4 servings

Don't be suspicious of the fish sauce. Although it is aggressively aromatic straight from the bottle, in this recipe the sauce loses its fishy smell when combined with the honey and spices. Serve with steamed rice to sop up the deliciously rich sauce. This recipe needs 1 to 2 hours of marinating time and about 1½ hours of cooking time, so be sure to plan ahead.

1½ pounds beef chuck or round, fat trimmed, cut into 2-inch cubes

¼ cup Asian fish sauce

¼ cup honey

1 teaspoon Sriracha or other hot sauce

1 clove garlic, grated

1 teaspoon grated fresh ginger

½ teaspoon Chinese five-spice powder

2 tablespoons extra-virgin olive oil

½ cup chopped yellow onion

1 clove garlic, chopped

1 to 2 cups beef or chicken broth

5 pieces whole star anise

2 stalks lemongrass, green tops trimmed, white parts cut into 2-inch pieces and halved lengthwise, or 2 strips lemon zest

1 cinnamon stick

1 cup carrot, cut into ¼-inch pieces

5 ounces snow peas, ends and strings pulled

4 cups cooked rice, for serving

1. Place the beef cubes in a large bowl and add the fish sauce, honey, Sriracha, grated garlic, ginger, and five-spice powder. Stir to combine. Cover and refrigerate for 1 to 2 hours.

2. When ready to cook the stew, heat 1 tablespoon of the olive oil in a Dutch oven or heavy braising pan over medium-high heat. Use tongs to add the meat, reserving the marinade. Cook for about 5 minutes over medium-high heat, turning the meat until evenly browned. Turn the heat to high and add the marinade. Boil gently for about 5 minutes, or until the marinade is reduced by half.

$3.$ While the meat is browning, heat the remaining 1 tablespoon of oil in a small skillet until hot enough to sizzle a piece of onion. Add the onion and cook, stirring, for about 5 minutes, or until golden brown. Add the chopped garlic and cook for 1 minute. Add to the browned meat.

$4.$ Add 1 cup of the broth, the star anise, lemongrass, and cinnamon stick to the meat. Heat until boiling. Decrease the heat to low, cover, and cook for about 1½ hours, or until the meat is tender, adding more broth to keep the stew moist, if necessary.

$5.$ Add the carrot and cook covered for about 5 minutes, or until almost tender. Spread the snow peas on top of the meat and carrot, cover, and cook for 4 to 5 minutes, until crisp tender.

$6.$ Serve the meat and vegetables on rice with plenty of the flavorful juices spooned over the top.

Honey is absorbed immediately upon eating and for this reason is considered an excellent quick source of energy and a digestive aid.

stir-fried lamb, japanese eggplant, and red bell pepper with moroccan spices

Makes 4 servings

A drizzle of honey adds a bright, glistening sheen to this appealing stir-fry of lamb, eggplant, and red bell peppers. Spicy fresh chiles add the perfect hit of heat and add balance to the sweetness of the honey. For this stir-fry I prefer long, slender Japanese eggplants, but in a pinch Italian globe eggplants will work. The Moroccan spice blend *ras el hanout* is sold in Middle Eastern shops and some supermarkets. The flavor of *ras el hanout* varies from brand to brand, but all are slightly sweet from allspice, cinnamon, and cardamom and pungent from black pepper, saffron, ginger, and turmeric.

¼ cup extra-virgin olive oil, plus more as needed

2 small Japanese eggplants, peeled and diced (about ½ inch)

1 teaspoon, plus 1 pinch coarse salt

Freshly ground black pepper

1 red bell pepper, diced (about ½ inch)

1 small onion, diced (about ½ inch)

1¼ pounds ground lamb

3 garlic cloves, grated

2 teaspoons Moroccan spice blend (*ras el hanout*)

1 teaspoon grated ginger

3 tablespoons honey

1 to 3 teaspoons minced jalapeño or serrano chile

2 tablespoons finely chopped cilantro (optional)

1. Set a wok or large heavy skillet over medium-high heat until hot enough to sizzle a drop of water. Place 3 tablespoons of the oil in the wok and swirl it to heat. Gradually add the eggplant, stirring constantly. Stir-fry over medium-high to high heat until the eggplant is browned. Drizzle the wok with additional oil as needed but refrain from using too much. Sprinkle with ½ teaspoon of salt and a generous grinding of pepper and transfer to a dish.

2. Add the remaining 1 tablespoon of oil to the wok and swirl to heat. Add the pepper and onion and cook, stirring. Adjust the heat between medium and medium-high until the pepper is wilted and the onion is golden. Sprinkle with the pinch of salt and a grinding of pepper. Transfer to the bowl with the eggplant.

3. Crumble the lamb into the wok. Break the meat into small clumps with a spatula and stir until it loses its pink color. Add the garlic, Moroccan spice blend, ginger, ½ teaspoon of salt, and a generous grinding of black pepper. Stir-fry for 5 minutes over medium heat.

4. Return the eggplant, pepper, and onion to the wok. Add the honey and chile, and stir-fry for about 1 minute to blend. Sprinkle with the cilantro.

Experiment with different varieties in this big-flavored stew. I have tried it with a prized leatherwood from Tasmania, chestnut honey from Tuscany, and my favorite local wildflower honey. Each adds a slightly different taste.

lamb and dried fig tagine

Makes 4 servings

This Moroccan spiced lamb stew fills the kitchen with the most fabulous aromas. It uses *ras el hanout*, which is sold in many markets as Moroccan spice blend. Use any dried fruit in place of the figs, if preferred. Apricots, dates, and prunes will become soft, absorb the flavorful juices, and add their own sweet flavor to the finished dish. The honey adds a bit of sweetness as well as a lovely sheen to the sauce.

2 tablespoons extra-virgin olive oil

1 cup chopped onion

1 teaspoon Moroccan spice blend (*ras el hanout*)

½ teaspoon ground turmeric

½ teaspoon ground cinnamon

1½ to 2 pounds lamb sirloin, trimmed and cubed (1 inch)

½ teaspoon salt

Freshly ground black pepper

1 (15-ounce) can diced tomatoes with juices

½ cup unsalted chicken broth

12 dried Mission figs, prunes, or apricots

1 cup carrot, cut into ½-inch pieces

2 tablespoons honey

1 tablespoon diced preserved lemon (page 129), or 1 teaspoon finely chopped lemon zest

2 tablespoons finely chopped cilantro

1. Heat the olive oil in a large Dutch oven or a braising pan. When it is hot enough to sizzle a piece of onion, add the onion, Moroccan spice blend, turmeric, and cinnamon. Cook, stirring, for about 5 minutes, or until the onions are translucent.

2. Add the lamb and sprinkle with the salt and a generous grinding of pepper. Cook the meat, turning, for about 5 minutes, or until lightly browned. Add the tomatoes and chicken broth and heat to boiling. Reduce the heat to low, cover, and cook for 30 minutes. Add the figs and carrot. Cover and cook for about 30 minutes longer, or until the meat is tender.

continued on page 98

3. Stir in the honey and lemon. If there is too much liquid, turn the heat to high and boil for about 5 minutes, or until the liquid is reduced. Taste the sauce and add more salt and pepper if needed. Sprinkle with cilantro and serve.

Honey is sweeter than table sugar. One teaspoon of honey has twenty-one calories. One teaspoon of sugar has sixteen calories.

I suggest orange blossom, tupelo, alfalfa, basswood, clover, or another mild honey with distinctive floral notes. But almost any mildly sweet honey will lend just the right sweetness to the sauce.

pork chops and apples with honey and apple cider sauce

Makes 4 servings

Pork with apples is a classic combination. The cider helps balance the sweetness of the apples and honey and makes a delicious light sauce that adds moisture to the meat. Pork is so lean these days, the only way to keep it tender is to cook it only until it is pale pink. Over-cooked pork becomes cardboard. The timing in the recipe is for chops almost an inch thick. If your chops are thinner, reduce the cooking time by 2 or 3 minutes.

4 boneless pork loin chops (¾ to 1 inch thick)

Coarse salt and freshly ground pepper

1 teaspoon chopped fresh rosemary

1 tablespoon extra-virgin olive oil

½ cup thin (⅛ inch) vertical slices onion

2 large apples, cored, quartered, and cut into ¼-inch slices

¼ cup honey

¼ cup apple cider vinegar

1. Sprinkle the pork lightly on both sides with salt, pepper, and ½ teaspoon of the rosemary. Set aside.

2. Heat the olive oil over medium heat in a large skillet, tilting the pan to coat the surface evenly. Place the onion in the skillet and cook, stirring, over low heat for about 3 minutes, or until wilted. Push the onion to the center of the skillet and put the pork chops around the edges. Turn the heat to medium or medium-high and brown the pork chops for 2 minutes on each side.

3. Add the apples, honey, and cider, and heat until the liquid boils. Cook, stirring the fruit and onion and turning the pork chops to coat with the boiling liquid, over medium-high heat for 5 minutes.

4. Transfer the pork to a serving platter. Spoon the apples and onion on top, and pour the juices in the pan over the top. Sprinkle with the remaining ½ teaspoon of rosemary.

I prefer a dark, big-flavored honey such as buckwheat, leatherwood, or mesquite, but any type of table honey will lend the sweetness needed to balance the acid of the vinegar and the heat of the chipotle.

baby back ribs with chipotle honey barbecue sauce

Makes 4 servings

Succulent and meaty baby back ribs are the perfect finger food. Although the honey helps temper the heat of the chipotle, it is best to use this fiery pepper sparingly. A can of chipotles packed in adobo sauce contains too many to use in one recipe. Select what you need and freeze the remaining. I find it useful to first discard the stems and puree the chiles and sauce, measure by the tablespoon, and freeze to use in bean soups, salad dressings, or stews.

Sauce

1 cup honey

1 cup ketchup

½ cup apple cider vinegar

2 tablespoons reduced-sodium soy sauce or tamari

2 canned chipotle chiles in adobo sauce, stems trimmed, chopped

2 tablespoons adobo sauce (from the can of chiles)

2 teaspoons chili powder

1 teaspoon ground cumin

1 teaspoon grated fresh garlic

1 teaspoon coarse salt

Ribs

2 racks (about 2½ pounds each) baby back ribs, each rack halved

Coarse salt and freshly ground black pepper

1. To make the sauce, place the honey, ketchup, vinegar, soy sauce, chipotles, adobo sauce, chili powder, cumin, garlic, and salt in a small saucepan. Heat on medium-low heat until simmering. Cook, uncovered, for 5 minutes. Let cool.

2. Season the ribs on both sides with a sprinkling of salt and a grinding of black pepper and rub in. Place the ribs in a 2-gallon, resealable plastic food storage bag and add the cooled sauce. Refrigerate for 4 to 24 hours, turning the bag occasionally.

continued on page 102

3. When ready to cook the ribs, preheat the oven to 350°F. Line a large roasting pan or a rimmed sheet pan with aluminum foil for easy cleanup. Fit a rack in the pan and place the ribs on the rack. Pour the sauce into a saucepan and gently heat over medium heat for 5 minutes. Brush the ribs with the sauce.

4. Roast the ribs for 1½ to 2 hours, basting lightly and turning every 20 minutes, until the meat begins to pull away from the bones. The ribs can be made ahead and left to stand for up to 2 hours either in a cool kitchen or in the refrigerator.

5. Preheat the broiler on high. Brush the ribs lightly with the sauce and broil for about 2 minutes, or until browned and bubbly. Cut between the ribs and pile them on a platter. Heat the leftover sauce to a gentle boil and simmer for 3 minutes before serving with the ribs.

{ TYPE OF HONEY } *Looking more for sweetness than a distinctive flavor, I tend to use orange blossom or clover honey for this marinade.*

pork tenderloin in tangerine, honey, and soy marinade

Makes 4 to 6 servings

Quickly browned in a skillet and then oven roasted, pork tenderloin takes on a glistening mahogany glaze with the distinctive taste of honey-sweetened tangerine. I keep a pair of pork tenderloins at the ready in the freezer. They thaw and roast quickly, making a delicious meal.

1 tangerine

2 pork tenderloins (1 to 1¼ pounds each)

3 tablespoons honey

2 tablespoons soy sauce or tamari

1 teaspoon grated fresh ginger

1 teaspoon toasted Asian sesame oil

½ teaspoon coarse salt

¼ teaspoon crushed red pepper

1. Use a vegetable peeler to remove the orange portion of the peel from half of the tangerine. Finely chop enough of the peel to measure 2 teaspoons. Halve the tangerine and squeeze the juice into a measuring cup. Reserve ¼ cup for the marinade.

2. Place the tenderloins in a heavy-duty, resealable plastic bag. Add the 2 teaspoons of tangerine peel, tangerine juice, honey, soy sauce, ginger, sesame oil, salt, and red pepper. Press excess air from the bag and seal. Massage the marinade into the meat and let it stand at room temperature for about 20 minutes or refrigerate up to 2 hours. If refrigerated, let it stand at room temperature for 30 minutes before cooking.

3. Preheat oven to 450°F. Heat a large heavy skillet over medium-high heat until hot enough to sizzle a drop of water. Brush lightly with olive oil. Lift the pork from the marinade and put in the hot skillet, adjusting heat to avoid excess splattering. Reserve the marinade. Cook the tenderloins about 30 seconds per side, turning with tongs as they brown.

continued on page 104

4. If using an iron or other ovenproof skillet, pour the marinade into a separate small skillet and bring to a boil. The marinade will thicken. Turn off the heat and brush the tops of the tenderloins with half of the marinade. If not using an ovenproof skillet, transfer the meat to a foil-lined roasting pan. Pour the marinade into the skillet and heat to a boil. Brush the tops of the tenderloins with half of the thickened marinade.

5. Put the tenderloins in the oven and roast for 8 minutes. Remove from the oven, turn with tongs, and baste with the remaining marinade. Return to the oven and roast for 7 to 8 minutes more, until an instant-read thermometer registers between 135°F and 140°F or meat is medium rare.

6. Let the tenderloins stand for 5 minutes. Transfer to a cutting board and cut into ¼-inch slices.

Because the delicate nuances of flavor in most varietal honey would be lost in this robust peanut sauce, I use more neutral-flavored clover, alfalfa, or orange blossom.

cold chinese noodles with spicy honey peanut sauce

Makes 4 servings

Peanut sauce for Chinese noodles is a favorite at our house. Instead of sugar, I add honey, which lends a smoother, more rounded sweetness to this addictive sauce. I like to add plenty of vegetables, such as scallions, carrots, and cucumbers, to the noodles.

1 pound fresh wheat-flour Chinese noodles or dried thin spaghetti

4 tablespoons toasted Asian sesame oil

4 tablespoons soy sauce

⅓ cup smooth peanut butter

¼ cup honey

3 tablespoons Chinese sesame paste

3 tablespoons unseasoned Japanese rice vinegar

2 to 4 tablespoons warm water

½ teaspoon coarse salt

¼ to ½ teaspoon crushed red pepper

3 scallions, cut into thin diagonal slices (green and white parts)

1 large carrot, coarsely shredded

½ crisp seedless cucumber, cut into thin strips (¼ by 1 inch)

2 tablespoons finely chopped cilantro

1. Heat a large pot half filled with water to boiling. Place the noodles in the water and cook, for about 4 minutes for fresh noodles and 8 minutes for dried spaghetti, or until tender. Drain well and rinse with cold water, lifting the cooked noodles with tongs to prevent sticking. Shake in a colander to remove excess water. Put the noodles in a large bowl. Add 2 tablespoons each of the sesame oil and the soy sauce. Refrigerate for about 1 hour.

2. To make the peanut sauce, combine the remaining 2 tablespoons each of sesame oil and soy sauce, peanut butter, honey, sesame paste, vinegar, 2 tablespoons of warm water, salt, and red pepper in a blender or the bowl of a food processor. Blend or process until the sauce is smooth. Taste and adjust the seasoning with more salt and red pepper, if desired.

continued on page 106

Adjust the thickness of the sauce with more warm water, adding it 1 tablespoon at a time, if needed. Set aside at room temperature.

3. When the noodles are chilled, add the peanut sauce and toss with tongs to distribute evenly. Spread the noodles on a deep platter and top with the scallions, carrots, cucumber, and cilantro.

Quick Hits: Main Dishes

- Drizzle equal parts of honey and lemon juice and 1 clove of garlic, grated, on sautéed seasoned chicken cutlets and cook for an additional 1 to 2 minutes, turning until juices are thickened.

- Drizzle a bowl of pumpkin or sweet potato soup with a dark rich buckwheat, pumpkin blossom, wildflower, or chestnut honey.

- Combine 1 tablespoon each of honey, soy, or tamari; 1 teaspoon of grated ginger; and a pinch of crushed red pepper as a marinade for shrimp, chicken tenders, or pork or beef stir-fry.

- Combine equal parts of a bold-tasting honey such as buckwheat or mesquite with orange or lemon juice and brush on grilled or roasted chicken or fish.

- Pan-sauté thick, boneless pork chops until medium rare. Drizzle with a mixture of 1 tablespoon each of honey and balsamic vinegar. Cook, turning the chops, until they are cooked to desired doneness and the honey has caramelized.

- Add honey along with soy sauce and unseasoned Japanese rice vinegar to fried rice or stir-fried dishes.

- Drizzle clover, orange blossom, or star thistle honey on corn fritters.

- Season lamb chops with finely chopped rosemary, coarse salt, and freshly ground pepper. Broil, brushing each side 1 minute before turning with a generous coating of your favorite honey mixed with a teaspoon of Dijon mustard.

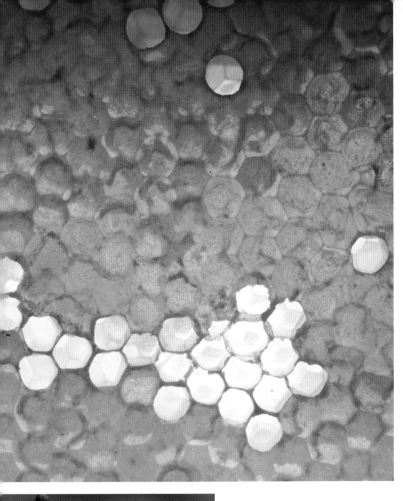

salads and vegetable side dishes

"I eat my peas with honey;
I've done it all my life.
It makes the peas taste funny,
But it keeps them on the knife."

—Anonymous

A bold-tasting, amber-hued wildflower honey works well with the tang of the cranberries and the heat of the ginger. But, if you're lucky enough to find cranberry honey, this is the place to use it.

cranberry, apple, and ginger-honey relish

Makes about 2 cups

I developed this delicious recipe for Thanksgiving, but I find myself making it to serve with chicken or turkey throughout the year. A riff on the classic raw cranberry, whole orange (rind and all), and lots of sugar recipe, this dish uses honey instead of sugar and adds ginger for a refreshing bite. Spoon it over slices of warm turkey, slather it on turkey sandwiches, or mix with mayonnaise and use it to flavor turkey or chicken salad.

12 ounces raw cranberries, rinsed and sorted (about 3 cups)

1 large, tart green apple (Pippin or under-ripe Granny Smith), quartered, cored, and cut into 1-inch chunks

2 tablespoons peeled, coarsely chopped fresh ginger

½ cup honey

1. Combine all of the ingredients in the bowl of a food processor and pulse until finely chopped.

2. Transfer to a storage container, cover tightly, and refrigerate for at least 2 hours, until macerated. The relish keeps for up to 1 week and only gets better as it stands.

{ TYPE OF HONEY } *Use a fruity honey such as orange blossom, tupelo, clover, basswood, or acacia, which contributes a mellow honey flavor and sweetness.*

shredded cabbage with creamy toasted cumin, honey, lime, and jalapeño dressing

Makes 4 servings

This simple salad is a close relative of coleslaw, thanks to the addition of mayonnaise to the dressing. Spiked with a jalapeño and mellowed with honey, the dressing is perfectly spicy with a hint of sweet.

Dressing

1 teaspoon ground cumin

3 tablespoons mayonnaise

3 tablespoons fresh lime juice

2 tablespoons honey

½ teaspoon coarse salt

½ teaspoon finely grated lime zest

Salad

5 cups (about 16 ounces) finely shredded cabbage

1 medium-size carrot, coarsely shredded (about ½ cup)

1 jalapeño, trimmed, halved, seeded, and cut into thin crosswise slices

1. Place the cumin in a small, heavy skillet and slowly warm on low heat, shaking the pan, for about 1 minute, or until fragrant. Let cool.

2. In a large serving bowl, whisk the mayonnaise, lime juice, honey, salt, lime zest, and toasted cumin.

3. Add the cabbage, carrots, and jalapeño and toss with tongs. For crispy cabbage, serve at once. For wilted cabbage and a creamier mixture, store the salad, covered, in the refrigerator for at least 1 hour before serving.

TYPE OF HONEY *I prefer a mildly floral, unassertive honey such as orange blossom, clover, acacia, or alfalfa in this simple dressing.*

chopped endive, apple, raisin, and toasted walnut salad with honey-lemon mayonnaise

Makes 4 servings

Chopped Belgian endive—small, spearlike heads of closely packed, crunchy pale green and white leaves—gives this classic apple, raisin, and walnut salad a welcome spark. The mayonnaise dressing made with lemon juice and honey requires no oil. I use Meyer lemons, which are much less acidic than other lemon varieties. If you don't have access to Meyer lemons, taste the dressing before adding the apples and other ingredients. If the dressing is too acidic, increase the honey and mayonnaise in ½ tablespoon increments until the taste is to your liking.

1 cup broken walnuts

Dressing

3 tablespoons fresh lemon juice

3 tablespoons honey

3 tablespoons mayonnaise

½ teaspoon coarse salt

Salad

2 to 3 heads endive, stems trimmed

2 cups crisp apples (2 to 3 apples), quartered, cored, and diced (about ⅓ inch)

½ cup celery, trimmed and diced (¼ inch)

½ cup raisins

1. Preheat the oven to 350°F. Spread the walnuts in a shallow pan and toast, about 10 minutes. Set aside.

2. Place the lemon juice, honey, mayonnaise, and salt in a large bowl and whisk until blended. Taste and add more honey and mayonnaise by ½ tablespoon increments as needed.

3. Halve the endive lengthwise and cut each half into ⅓-inch-wide lengthwise spears. Gather the spears and cut crosswise into ⅓-inch pieces. Add the endive, apples, celery, raisins, and walnuts to the dressing. Toss to coat. Serve chilled or at room temperature.

I prefer a mild honey with distinctive floral notes such as thyme, star thistle, orange or lemon blossom, tupelo, or acacia.

all-purpose honey mustard salad dressing

Makes about ⅔ cup

A friend and great cook, Debbie Rugh, inspired me to make this simple salad dressing. We love it on crisp cooked asparagus, sliced beet salad, or tossed salad greens.

5 tablespoons extra-virgin olive oil

2 tablespoons full-bodied red wine vinegar

2 tablespoons honey

2 teaspoons Dijon mustard

1 small clove garlic, grated

½ teaspoon coarse salt

Freshly ground black pepper

1. Combine all of the ingredients in a blender and blend until emulsified. If making by hand, combine all of the ingredients except the olive oil in a small deep bowl. Add the olive oil a few drops at a time, continuously whisking until emulsified.

2. Store in a glass jar at room temperature for up to 1 day or refrigerate and keep for up to 1 week.

{ TYPE OF HONEY } *A light-colored, mildly flavored honey is best. Select from clover, alfalfa, lime or lemon blossom, raspberry, tupelo, or acacia.*

mango and celery salad with honey and lime dressing

Makes 4 to 6 servings

This is a pretty and delicious side dish "salsa," or a chopped salad to serve with grilled fish, chicken, or pork. The recipe is easily halved, but it is so refreshing I find myself making the full recipe and never having leftovers.

½ cup mayonnaise

2 tablespoons honey

2 tablespoons fresh lime juice

½ teaspoon finely grated lime zest

Pinch of coarse salt

2 ripe mangoes, halved, peeled, pitted, and diced (¼ inch)

1 cup diced celery (¼ inch)

½ cup sliced scallions (green and white parts) (¼ inch)

1 tablespoon chopped mint or cilantro (optional)

1. Place the mayonnaise, honey, lime juice, lime zest, and salt in a serving bowl and whisk until well blended.

2. Add the mangoes, celery, scallions, and mint. Fold to moisten with the dressing. Serve at room temperature or chilled.

I prefer to use a light-colored, mild-tasting honey such as clover, orange blossom, or alfalfa in this spicy dressing.

chicken and apple salad with curried honey mayonnaise

Makes 2 servings as a main dish and 4 as a side dish

To maximize the exotic taste of curry and other spices it helps to first warm them in a skillet. It is an easy step that takes less than a minute and makes a world of difference in the depth of flavor. A bit of honey stirred into the jalapeño and Madras curry–spiced mayonnaise tempers its spiciness and adds balance. You might wish to use seedless grapes in place of the apples and during stone fruit season substitute chunks of firm ripe peaches or nectarines.

1½ teaspoons Madras curry powder

½ cup mayonnaise

1 tablespoon fresh lemon or lime juice

1 tablespoon minced jalapeño

½ teaspoon coarse salt (optional)

Pinch of cayenne pepper (optional)

2 to 3 cups diced cooked chicken

1 crisp apple, quartered, cored, and diced (¼ inch)

½ cup diced celery (¼ inch)

¼ cup minced sweet onion

½ cup coarsely chopped roasted unsalted cashews (optional)

1. Place the curry in a small dry skillet and set over low heat, shaking the pan, for about 1 minute, or until the curry is warm and fragrant. Remove the pan from the heat and let stand until cooled. Add the mayonnaise to the cooled pan and stir to combine thoroughly with the curry. Stir in the lemon juice, jalapeño, salt, and cayenne (if you want extra heat) until blended.

2. In a large bowl, combine the chicken, apple, celery, and onion. Add the mayonnaise and fold until thoroughly blended. Sprinkle with cashews.

I prefer a deep-flavored, amber-hued honey that will stand out in the heady mixture of assertive flavors in this salad. My choices include complex wildflower honey with hints of fennel, a richly floral sunflower with hints of vanilla, a spicy goldenrod, or a buttery avocado.

pear, stilton, and bacon salad with honey-glazed pecans

Makes 4 servings

I discovered years ago when writing a healthy-cooking column that an easy way to cut the fat in salad dressing was to substitute honey for the oil. As much as I love olive oil, there are times when it might not be totally necessary for the overall balance in a dish, especially when the recipe has other ingredients that lend that fatty mouthfeel. In this salad, that is provided by the Stilton cheese and crumbled bacon. The dressing is simply a mixture of red wine vinegar and honey whisked with a bit of coarse salt. It is necessary to build this salad on a platter, carefully arranging the ingredients so they retain their integrity. The glazed nuts make a great snack, so you might want to double the ingredients. Walnuts or another nut can be used in place of the pecans, if desired.

Honey-Glazed Pecans

½ cup broken pecans

1 tablespoon honey

½ teaspoon coarse salt

Freshly ground black pepper

Dressing

3 tablespoons honey

3 tablespoons red wine vinegar

½ teaspoon coarse salt

1 large or 2 small ripe Bartlett, Anjou, or Bosc pears, quartered, cored, and sliced ¼ inch thick

4 cups torn mixed salad greens

2 slices bacon, crisp cooked and crumbled

4 ounces (about 1 cup) Stilton, cut into small cubes or crumbled

1. To make the honey-glazed pecans, tear off a 10-inch sheet of aluminum foil. Place the nuts in a small skillet and heat over medium heat, stirring, until hot. Decrease the heat to low and drizzle with the honey. Cook, stirring and adjusting the heat as needed to boil the honey. Cook for 2 to 3 minutes, until the honey has coated the nuts and they begin to caramelize. Spread the nuts on the foil. Sprinkle with the salt and a grinding of black pepper. Set aside to cool.

continued on page 119

$2.$ To make the dressing, whisk the honey, vinegar, and salt in a large bowl until well blended.

$3.$ Place the sliced pears in a separate bowl and add 2 tablespoons of the dressing. Reserve the remaining dressing for the greens.

$4.$ Add the salad greens to the large bowl with the remaining dressing and toss to coat. Spread the dressed salad greens on a serving platter or in a large shallow bowl. Top with the crumbled bacon and the Stilton. Arrange the pears around the edges and pour any dressing left in the bowl over the top of the salad. Break the pecans into pieces and use to garnish the salad.

Variation:

Instead of using bacon, substitute four slices of prosciutto, cut into 1-inch pieces. Have ready a strainer set over a heatproof bowl. Heat ¼ inch of olive oil in a small skillet until hot enough to sizzle a piece of the prosciutto. Add the remaining prosciutto and cook, stirring, over medium heat for about 30 seconds, or until it is crisped and "frizzled." Pour the contents of the skillet into the strainer. Reserve the oil for another use. Sprinkle the prosciutto over the salad.

> Honey vinegar is made by fermenting honey and water and is delicious on salads and in recipes that use fruit vinegar.

{ TYPE OF HONEY }

I prefer a slightly herbaceous honey such as star thistle with notes of mint or spice, a full-bodied orange blossom, or a rich amber-colored wildflower. If you have a thyme or oregano honey, use it here and add a shower of fresh chopped thyme or oregano leaves to heighten the herb flavor.

roasted red onion wedges with honey and balsamic vinegar

Makes 4 servings

Roasted onions take longer to cook than sautéed onions, but because the natural sweetness of the onion is preserved it is worth the wait. Once the onions are roasted, a drizzle of honey and a bit of balsamic vinegar turn them from prosaic to sophisticated.

6 medium-size (about 2½ inches in diameter) red onions, peeled and cut into ½-inch wedges (about 4 cups)

2 tablespoons extra-virgin olive oil

½ teaspoon coarse salt

⅛ teaspoon freshly ground black pepper

2 tablespoons honey

1½ teaspoons balsamic vinegar

1 tablespoon finely chopped fresh dill or mint

1 teaspoon chopped fresh oregano or thyme (optional)

1. Preheat the oven to 400°F. Place the onions in a 9- or 10-inch pie plate or baking dish. Drizzle with the oil and 1 tablespoon of water and sprinkle with the salt and pepper. Cover tightly with aluminum foil and oven braise for 30 minutes.

2. Remove the dish from the oven, uncover, and drizzle the onions with the honey. Return to the oven and roast uncovered, stirring once or twice, for 20 to 25 minutes, until the onions are fork tender and turning golden brown around the edges of the dish.

3. Add a few drops of the balsamic vinegar on the onions to taste. Sprinkle with dill and the other herbs.

Use a neutral-flavored honey such as an orange blossom or clover in this boldly flavored dish.

cabbage and carrot stir-fry with honey and peanuts

Makes 4 servings

Cabbage, available already shredded and ready to use, is an easy choice for a quick vegetable or salad. Here cabbage and coarsely shredded carrots (also readily available) are used in a quick stir-fried side dish. The honey in this recipe adds a pleasant sweetness that balances big flavors from the vinegar and sesame oil and heat from the generous amount of fresh ginger and the jalapeños.

¼ cup unseasoned Japanese rice vinegar

2 tablespoons honey

2 teaspoons toasted Asian sesame oil

2 tablespoons extra-virgin olive oil

1 tablespoon finely chopped fresh ginger

1 clove garlic, grated or finely chopped

1 package (10 ounces) shredded green cabbage, or 6 cups coarsely chopped or shredded cabbage

2 cups coarsely chopped or thickly shredded carrot

1 medium-size jalapeño, halved lengthwise, stem and seeds removed, thinly sliced

½ teaspoon coarse salt

½ cup coarsely chopped, lightly salted roasted peanuts

1. Whisk the vinegar, honey, and sesame oil in a small bowl. Set aside.

2. Combine the oil, ginger, and garlic in a wok or large skillet and heat on low for about 1 minute, or just until the garlic begins to sizzle. Add the cabbage, carrot, and jalapeño and stir-fry, over medium heat, for about 3 minutes, or until the vegetables are crisp-tender. Add the vinegar mixture and the salt, and stir-fry for 30 seconds, until well blended.

3. Transfer to a serving bowl and sprinkle with the peanuts.

Select a mild honey with floral notes or go another route and try this with a complex wildflower. Another choice is a cinnamon-infused honey, which is sometimes hard to find but delicious.

honey-glazed beets with cinnamon, orange, and mint

Makes 4 servings

A cinnamon stick simmered with the beets in a shallow pool of water gently perfumes the beets. I prefer to peel raw beets with a vegetable peeler and cut them into chunks before cooking. The smaller pieces will shorten the cooking time, and the cut surfaces allow greater opportunity for absorbing the spice.

1½ to 2 pounds beets (about 12 small or 8 medium-size beets), tops removed, peeled, halved or quartered

¾ cup water, plus extra if necessary

1 cinnamon stick

½ teaspoon coarse salt

2 tablespoons torn fresh mint leaves

1 strip (½ by 3-inches) orange zest, cut into long thin strips

1 clove garlic, bruised with the side of a knife

3 tablespoons honey

Freshly ground black pepper

1. Place the beets and ¾ cup of water in a heavy 10- to 12-inch skillet with a lid. Add the cinnamon stick and salt and bring to a boil. Cover and simmer over low heat for about 20 minutes, or until the beets are tender when poked with the tip of a knife. Check the water level from time to time, adding 2 tablespoons at a time if the pan is getting dry. When the beets are tender, remove the lid, and if there is still water in the skillet turn the heat to medium-high and boil until the water is evaporated.

2. While the beets are cooking, gather the mint, orange, and garlic together in a pile and chop finely. Set aside.

3. Drizzle the cooked beets with the honey and stir over medium heat until the honey boils and coats the beets. Add a grinding of pepper. Sprinkle with the mint mixture.

Almost any honey with a subtle herbaceous flavor will work in this recipe, but I like to use an oregano, thyme, or rosemary—all from my well-stocked honey pantry—to match the herb I'm using to garnish the carrots.

honey-glazed carrots with oregano

Makes 4 servings

If you are fortunate enough to shop a farmers' market or a market that sells small, slender carrots, then this recipe is perfect. If all you can find are large carrots, trim them to one size and halve or quarter each one for even cooking.

1 pound slender carrots, scrubbed, peeled (if necessary), and trimmed (see headnote)

2 tablespoons extra-virgin olive oil

1 tablespoon fresh oregano, thyme, or rosemary leaves, chopped

Coarse salt

3 tablespoons honey

1 tablespoon fresh lemon juice

1. Place the carrots in a single layer in a large skillet with a lid. Drizzle with olive oil and sprinkle with half of the herb leaves of choice and about ½ teaspoon of salt. Cook covered over low heat for 10 to 15 minutes, turning occasionally, until the carrots are almost tender.

2. Drizzle with the honey and cook uncovered for about 5 minutes, turning with a fork until the honey thickens and coats the carrots and they begin to caramelize. Remove from the heat. Splash with the lemon juice, sprinkle with the remaining half of the preferred herb leaves, and serve.

I have tried this recipe with a wide variety of honeys. Clover, orange blossom, and alfalfa, the workhorse honeys in my kitchen, are good choices. But I also like the more distinctive flavor of dark amber wildflower or buckwheat, or a light-hued complex floral tupelo or sourwood.

honey and cumin roasted sweet potato rounds

Makes 4 servings

Sweet potatoes are a great canvas for a wide variety of spices, but my new favorite is ground cumin. Cumin is an ancient spice that dates to the Old Testament. The crescent-shaped seeds are the dried fruit of a plant related to parsley. The seeds are used whole or ground and can be found in curry, chili, and many Asian, Middle Eastern, and other cuisines. Almost any variety of sweet potatoes works in this recipe, although I am partial to the creamy, deep orange Beauregard or Garnet.

1 teaspoon ground cumin	2 tablespoons extra-virgin olive oil
½ teaspoon coarse salt	4 tablespoons honey
2 large sweet potatoes, scrubbed and cut into ½-inch-thick rounds	

1. Preheat the oven to 400°F. Combine the cumin and salt in a small bowl and set aside.

2. Place the sweet potato rounds in a bowl, drizzle with the olive oil, and toss to coat evenly. Arrange the sweet potatoes in a single layer on a rimmed sheet pan. Brush with 2 tablespoons of the honey and sprinkle with half of the cumin salt.

3. Roast for 25 minutes. Remove the pan from the oven and turn the sweet potatoes. Brush with the remaining 2 tablespoons of the honey and sprinkle with the remaining cumin salt. Roast for about 20 minutes, or until the potatoes are tender and browned.

This is a great place to show off your most fragrant, interesting honey varieties. I love it with sage, rosemary, or oregano honey, but star thistle, wildflower, and many others will come through loud and clear as well.

chunky butternut squash and apple with honey

Makes 4 servings

This unusual combination of squash cooked with chunks of apple and roughly mashed with honey and butter is amazing and addictive. Add a pinch of a favorite spice if you are so inclined, but I love it best plain and simple. Because I find prepping butternut squash cumbersome, I've come up with the method described in the recipe.

1 butternut squash (1½ to 2 pounds), halved, seeded, and cut into 2- or 3-inch chunks

2 crisp apples, peeled, quartered, cored, and cut into ½-inch chunks

2 tablespoons unsalted butter

2 tablespoons honey

½ teaspoon coarse salt

1 teaspoon minced fresh herb leaves to match the honey (optional)

1. Place the squash in a steamer set over an inch or more of boiling water. Cover and steam for 15 minutes, until almost tender. Add the apples to the squash, cover, and steam for about 15 minutes longer, or until the squash and apples are fork tender.

2. Let cool slightly. Select the chunks of squash from the steamer. Scoop the squash flesh from the skins, or if preferred cut the skin from the flesh with a paring knife. Transfer the peeled squash and the apples to a large saucepan.

3. Add the butter and honey, and with a potato masher or a big wooden spoon, roughly mash the squash and apples, leaving some chunks of each. Add the salt. Sprinkle with the fresh herb of choice.

Use an amber-hued honey with bright notes of mint and other herbs. Perhaps a late-summer wildflower honey with fennel notes, a buttery-rich safflower, or a deeply herbal leatherwood with notes of butterscotch. But in a pinch almost any favorite honey, as long as it's not too delicate or subtle, will do very well.

moroccan-style stewed tomatoes and fennel with honey and preserved lemon

Makes 6 or more servings as a side dish

This is called a cooked salad in Moroccan cuisine and is typically part of an extensive menu of other cooked vegetable dishes served room temperature at the start of a Moroccan meal. Scooped up with chunks of bread (never forks), these dishes are always heady with spices, herbs, and great flavors. This dish was inspired by a recipe from Mourad Lahlou, the chef at Aziza, a Moroccan restaurant in San Francisco. The addition of honey and preserved lemon may not be traditional, but they offer a pleasant contrast of sweet and salty to this complex dish.

¼ cup extra-virgin olive oil

2 cups chopped yellow onion

1 fennel bulb, tops and thick green stems trimmed, quartered, core removed, sliced thinly

1 cup thinly sliced celery

2 tablespoons coarsely chopped garlic

1 teaspoon fennel seeds

1 teaspoon coarse salt

¼ teaspoon coarsely ground black pepper

⅛ teaspoon crushed red pepper

1 (28-ounce) can plum tomatoes with juices

¼ cup apple cider vinegar or honey vinegar

¼ cup raisins

1 tablespoon finely chopped rind of preserved lemon, or 1 teaspoon finely chopped lemon zest (see note)

3 to 4 tablespoons honey

1. Heat the oil in a large sauté pan or deep skillet with a lid until hot enough to sizzle a piece of onion. Add the onion, fennel, and celery and reduce the heat to low. Cover and braise for 5 minutes.

2. Meanwhile, mash the garlic, fennel seeds, salt, black pepper, and red pepper with a mortar and pestle. If you don't have a mortar and pestle, grate the garlic into a bowl; chop the fennel seeds with a large knife, then combine the garlic, fennel seeds, salt, black and red pepper in a small bowl, mashing with the back of a spoon until blended.

3. Stir the mashed garlic mixture into the onion mixture and continue to braise, covered, on low heat for 10 to 15 minutes, until very soft but not browned.

4. Puree the tomatoes in a food processor or push through a food mill. Add the tomatoes, vinegar, and raisins to the onion mixture and heat to a boil. Cook, uncovered, over medium-low heat for about 15 minutes, or until the tomatoes are cooked down and the mixture is thickened.

5. Add the preserved lemon and honey and heat through. Serve at room temperature with sliced meats, or warm as a side dish with roast lamb or over hot rice, quinoa pilaf, or cooked white beans.

Note: *Preserved lemons are a staple in a Moroccan pantry. They are simply lemons cut into quarters, coated heavily with coarse salt, and packed into a jar with lemon juice to cover. The ratio is 3 small lemons to ¼ cup of coarse salt and about ½ cup of fresh lemon juice. The lemons need to mature for at least 2 weeks before they are ready to use. Jars of preserved lemons are available in many specialty food shops and online (see Sources).*

> Because of its concentration of sugar and low percentage of water, pure honey is an excellent preservative. Undiluted honey should be stored at room temperature and will never spoil or ferment.

I like a slightly astringent, bold-tasting honey to counter the creamy feta but also one that stands up to the tang of the roasted eggplant. My choices are eucalyptus, pine or fir, firewood, or star thistle, but any earthy, aromatic honey is excellent. You might also wish to use a honey to match the thyme or oregano used to garnish the dish.

roasted eggplant slices with warmed feta and honey drizzle

Makes 4 servings

A restaurant review describing fried eggplant slices topped with pecorino cheese curls and drizzled with honey was the inspiration for this unlikely combination. I roasted the eggplant instead of frying it and crumbled a mild feta on top before drizzling with honey. The results were so dazzling my tasters raved as they helped themselves to more. Look for a creamy and mild, nonsalty feta. Typically French feta is quite mild, but I recently discovered a sweet, creamy sheep's milk feta from Israel.

1 large eggplant, about 1¼ pounds

6 tablespoons extra-virgin olive oil

1½ cups (about 8 ounces) crumbled mild-tasting feta cheese

Freshly ground black pepper

Approximately ½ cup honey, or as needed

1 tablespoon fresh thyme or oregano leaves, chopped, for garnish

1. Preheat the oven to 400°F. Trim each end from the eggplant. With a vegetable peeler, partially remove the skin in alternating wide strips, leaving the eggplant with a striped appearance. Cut the eggplant into ¾-inch-thick rounds.

2. Place the eggplant slices in rows on a rimmed sheet pan. Generously brush both sides of the slices with the olive oil.

3. Roast for 10 to 12 minutes, until the bottoms are lightly browned. Remove the pan from the oven and turn the slices with a wide spatula. Return the pan to the oven and roast for about 10 minutes longer, or until the eggplant is lightly browned and tender. Remove the pan from the oven and mound a rounded tablespoon of cheese on top of each eggplant slice. Add a grinding of black pepper to each. Return the pan to the oven for about 5 minutes, or until the cheese softens.

4. Transfer the slices to a serving platter. Drizzle each with the honey and sprinkle with a few fresh thyme leaves. Serve hot.

Honey and Bees in History and Legend

- Dating 50,000 years ago, amber found in the Baltic region contains fossilized bees.

- An 8,000-year-old rock painting in the Cave of the Spider near Valencia, Spain, is just one of several such paintings found throughout the world that depict the gathering of honey.

- Excavations of Egyptian tombs revealed beehives, evidence of bee-keeping activities.

- The Greek god Aristaeus, the son of Apollo, was the god of beekeeping. When the bees in the kingdom died, he was advised to sacrifice animals. From the carcasses came bees.

- Pliny the Elder, the Roman philosopher and naturalist (AD 23–79); Aristotle, the Greek philosopher (384–322 BC); and Columella, the Roman writer on agriculture (AD 4–70) wrote about bees. Virgil, the Roman poet (70–19 BC), wrote an entire volume of poems about bees and beekeeping.

- Honey was the first food of the Greek god Zeus. The Romans offered sacrifices of honey to appease Pluto, the god of the underworld.

- Ancients used honey and beeswax as an embalming liquid. It preserved bodies for hundreds of years. Alexander the Great is said to have been embalmed in honey.

- Ancient Egyptians used honey as money. Romans are said to have paid their taxes in honey.

- Early Greek and Germanic newlyweds licked honey off each other's hands to symbolize sharing food, kindness, and sweetness toward each other.

- Honey was thought to symbolize truth because it came from bees without needing to be transformed by people. The name "Deborah" is from Hebrew words for "bee" and "word," or "truth". An ancient Egyptian saying is, "Honey is the truth."

- Charles Butler asserted in *The Feminine Monarchie* (1609) that what until then was thought to be the king bee was actually a queen bee.

- François Huber (1750–1831), a blind Swiss naturalist who wrote *New Observations on the Natural History of Bees*, carried out his work with the aid of his observant wife.

Quick Hits: Salads and Vegetable Side Dishes

- Dress a lettuce salad with equal parts of fresh lemon juice and honey for a quick, oil-free salad dressing. Add ½ clove of garlic, grated, and a pinch of salt.

- Dress a fruit salad with equal parts of fresh lime juice and honey. Add grated ginger, if desired.

- Steam 2 cups of fresh peas or thawed frozen peas until tender. Stir in 1 tablespoon each of butter, honey, and finely chopped fresh mint. Serve steaming hot.

- Toss arugula leaves and olive oil and spread a thin layer on a serving plate. Remove the skin and pith from 3 seedless oranges and cut the oranges into thin rounds. Spread the orange slices on top of the arugula. Drizzle with orange blossom honey or other fruit blossom honey and sprinkle lightly with ground red pepper.

- Brush halved sweet potatoes with a thin glaze of buckwheat, sourwood, or basswood honey during the last few minutes of roasting, grilling, or broiling.

- Sauté thick wedges of apples, pears, figs, or firm ripe peaches in butter until slightly colored, drizzle with honey, and boil for about 1 minute, or until caramelized. Splash with balsamic, sherry, apple cider, or other fruit vinegar and sprinkle with chopped oregano or rosemary leaves. Serve warm with roasted pork, chicken, or lamb.

sweets

Baking with Honey

To ensure success when baking with honey, there are some guidelines that should be followed. Among them are the following:

- The high heat of baking tends to neutralize the distinctive flavor notes in varietal honey, so it is best to use mildly flavored honey such as orange blossom, clover, and alfalfa.

- Highly spiced batters and chocolate are an exception. In these recipes I like complex dark buckwheat, wildflower, pumpkin blossom, or whatever robustly flavored honey is on hand.

- Measure honey in solid metal or plastic measuring spoons or cups that have been brushed with flavorless vegetable oil or sprayed with nonstick cooking spray. The honey will slip right out.

- Honey is sold by weight, not volume. A 12-ounce jar of honey yields a standard 8-ounce measuring cup.

- When baking with honey, the eggs, butter, yogurt, milk, water, and other typically refrigerated or cool ingredients should be brought to room temperature first. If these ingredients are used while chilled, the batter will take on a curdled, instead of a smooth, appearance.

- To warm eggs, set them in a bowl and cover with very hot tap water. They'll warm up in about 10 minutes.

- Because honey is heavy, it sometimes falls to the bottom of the batter during baking. To avoid this, warm the honey over low heat until it is thinned but not hot, and thoroughly combine the batter ingredients by folding from the bottom with a wide rubber spatula.

- You can warm an entire glass jar of honey by standing it in a bowl or pan of very hot water or by placing it in a microwave-safe container and microwaving very briefly, 5 to 10 seconds. Generally, microwaving is not recommended, especially for raw honey, because it will destroy the pollen and other natural goodness, but the baking will do that anyway.

- Because batters made with honey tend to brown more readily, some recipes quickly bake at a slightly lower (25° to 50°F) oven temperature.

- Honey is hygroscopic (takes up and retains moisture) and keeps breads, cookies, and cakes moist for longer periods of time.

- Save your precious varietal or single-origin honey to use as a finishing touch by drizzling it on warm toast, over ice cream, or on grilled vegetables or fruits. Or use it in recipes for Honey Panna Cotta (page 171), Sweet Cheese Tart (page 153), or Honey Zabaglione (page 169), where the distinctive honey taste will be appreciated.

> Overheating honey can cause the destruction of many components, including antimicrobial compounds.

Use a favorite all-purpose honey. I usually reach for a clover or orange blossom honey when I make these.

honey oatmeal raisin cookies

Makes about 3 dozen small cookies

My friend and colleague Brooke Jackson lent me a dog-eared copy of a childhood treasure, *The Pooh Cook Book* by Virginia H. Ellison. The following cookie recipe is loosely adapted from this collection. The cookies are chewy rather than crumbly, and the taste of honey is dominant. I suspect that is why these are one of Pooh's favorite treats; that is, when he doesn't have his paw in his hunny jar.

½ cup firmly packed light brown sugar

¼ cup honey

¼ cup (½ stick) unsalted butter, softened

1 large egg, at room temperature

½ cup unbleached all-purpose flour

½ teaspoon coarse salt

¼ teaspoon baking soda, sifted

1½ cups old-fashioned oats

½ cup raisins

½ cup chopped walnuts

1. Preheat the oven to 325°F. Lightly coat two baking sheets with butter or nonstick cooking spray.

2. Place the brown sugar, honey, and butter in the large bowl of a stand mixer and beat for about 5 minutes, or until light and fluffy. Add the egg and beat until well blended.

3. In a separate bowl, stir together the flour, salt, and baking soda and then blend into the batter on low speed. Stir in the oatmeal, raisins, and walnuts with a wooden spoon or rubber spatula.

4. Drop the batter by rounded tablespoonfuls onto the baking sheets 1 inch apart. Bake for 15 to 18 minutes, until the bottoms are golden brown and the cookies are set. Let cool slightly and then transfer the cookies to a wire rack.

The peanut taste overwhelms the delicate flavors in most varietal honey, so I stick with everyday clover or orange blossom honey. If using other nuts, I suggest a dark, complex honey such as wildflower, sourwood, avocado, or golden rod. How about macadamia nut brittle made with macadamia honey?

salted honey peanut brittle

Makes 24 pieces

Chewy, peanuty, and salty, this confection is addictive. Break it into irregularly shaped morsels just the right size for a delicious mouthful. Wrap each bite in a square of waxed paper or plastic wrap so the morsels won't stick to each other. For a more sophisticated taste, try this with other nuts; toasted peeled hazelnuts are especially good.

4 tablespoons (½ stick) unsalted butter

¼ cup granulated sugar

¼ cup honey

¼ cup heavy cream

2 teaspoons coarse salt

1½ cups dry-roasted, lightly salted peanuts

1. Line a sheet pan with lightly buttered aluminum foil or a nonstick baking mat.

2. Combine the butter, sugar, honey, cream, and 1 teaspoon of the salt in a heavy-bottomed medium saucepan. Heat over medium-low, stirring, until the mixture comes to a boil. Boil, stirring frequently, over medium to medium-low heat for 4 to 5 minutes, until the mixture turns a deep amber color. Adjust the heat to maintain a steady boil and stir to keep the mixture from boiling over or scorching.

3. Stir in the peanuts and immediately scrape the mixture onto the lined sheet pan, spreading it in a single layer with a rubber spatula. Sprinkle the surface evenly with the remaining 1 teaspoon of salt.

4. Let the peanut brittle cool thoroughly for about 1 hour, or until hardened. Lift it from the pan and break into irregularly shaped pieces about ¾ inch across.

5. Cut waxed paper or plastic wrap into 2-inch squares and wrap each piece individually. Stored at room temperature in a cool, dry place, the brittle keeps indefinitely.

Use a light to amber honey, such as alfalfa or cloves, or an early summer golden wildflower blend. For a more distinctive taste, use a rich, complex buckwheat or a dark amber super-floral honey such as apple or pumpkin blossom, avocado, or sourwood.

honey and date-nut squares

Makes 16 squares

Part bar cookie and part cake, these are tender and sweet, moist and chewy. They are perfect with a midafternoon cup of tea or a glass of milk. They improve with age and freeze very well.

½ cup (1 stick) unsalted butter, softened

¼ cup firmly packed light brown sugar

1 large egg, at room temperature

½ teaspoon vanilla extract

½ cup honey, plus 2 tablespoons for glaze

1 cup plus 2 tablespoons unbleached all-purpose flour

1 teaspoon ground cinnamon

½ teaspoon baking powder, sifted

¼ teaspoon baking soda, sifted

⅓ cup chopped walnuts

⅓ cup chopped dates (¼ inch)

1. Preheat the oven to 350°F. Lightly coat a 9-inch square pan with butter or nonstick cooking spray.

2. Place the butter and brown sugar in the large bowl of a stand mixer and beat for about 5 minutes, or until light and fluffy. Add the egg and vanilla and beat until the mixture is smooth and fluffy. On slow speed, gradually beat in ½ cup of the honey until completely blended.

3. Sift together 1 cup of the flour, and the cinnamon, baking powder, and baking soda. Gradually stir the dry ingredients into the creamed mixture. In a separate bowl, toss the walnuts and dates with the remaining 2 tablespoons of flour. Fold into the batter.

4. Spread the batter in the pan and smooth the top with a spatula. Bake for about 25 minutes, or until the surface is golden and the edges are pulled away from the pan.

5. Meanwhile, place the remaining 2 tablespoons of honey in a custard cup or other small heatproof bowl. Warm the honey in the microwave for 5 seconds or place it in a pan of hot water until it is thinned.

6. While still warm, brush the date-nut squares with the thinned honey. Let cool thoroughly before cutting into squares.

chunky peanut butter and honey cookies

Makes about 3½ dozen

Nuts and honey seem to have an affinity for each other. It might be the fat of the nut and the sweetness of the honey, but whatever the attraction they are perfection in many recipes, from the simplest peanut butter and honey sandwich to the more complicated cookie. Chock-full of coarsely chopped dry-roasted peanuts and rich with the taste of chunky peanut butter and honey, these tender cookies cry out for a glass of cold milk.

½ cup (1 stick) unsalted butter, softened

½ cup chunky peanut butter

½ cup firmly packed light brown sugar

1 large egg, at room temperature

½ teaspoon vanilla extract

½ cup honey

1 cup unbleached all-purpose flour

½ cup whole wheat flour

½ teaspoon baking powder, sifted

½ teaspoon baking soda, sifted

½ teaspoon coarse salt

¾ cup coarsely chopped, unsalted dry-roasted peanuts

1. Arrange a rack in the top third of the oven. Preheat the oven to 325°F. Line two baking sheets with parchment paper or coat with nonstick cooking spray.

2. Place the butter, peanut butter, and brown sugar in the large bowl of a stand mixer and beat for about 5 minutes, or until light and fluffy. Beat in the egg and vanilla until the mixture is well blended. Beat in the honey in a slow, steady stream until blended.

3. Combine the flours, baking powder, baking soda, and salt in a small bowl. Gradually beat into the batter on slow speed until blended. Add the peanuts and stir in with a rubber spatula.

4. Drop the batter by rounded tablespoonfuls about 1½ inches apart. Bake one sheet at a time for 10 to 13 minutes, until the edges are browned, but the centers are soft. Let the cookies cool on the baking sheets before removing with a spatula. The centers will firm up as the cookies cool.

Variation:

For Chunky Peanut Butter and Chocolate Chip Cookies, decrease the amount of peanuts to ½ cup and add ½ cup of semisweet chocolate chips.

Honey contains small amounts of vitamins and minerals. The amounts will vary with the source of the nectar. Some compounds in honey are thought to function as antioxidants. Potassium is the most prominent mineral.

Not to be overwhelmed by the chocolate and espresso, I like to use a big-flavored wildflower, buckwheat, avocado, or eucalyptus honey that will complement the mix of flavors.

honey chocolate cake with chocolate-honey icing or honey whipped cream

Makes 8 servings

Moist and chocolaty with hints of espresso and honey, this is a favorite cake in our family. I served it with honey-sweetened whipped cream until our 3-year-old grandson, Joey, already a dedicated chocolate fan, insisted that it have chocolate icing. This delicate cake uses cake flour. To approximate cake flour when none is on hand, place 2 tablespoons of cornstarch in a 1-cup measure and add enough all-purpose flour to fill the cup. Stir well to blend.

4 squares (4 ounces) unsweetened chocolate

½ cup (1 stick) unsalted butter, softened

¾ cup firmly packed light brown sugar

½ cup honey

2 large eggs, at room temperature

1 teaspoon vanilla extract

2 cups sifted cake flour (see headnote for substitution)

1 teaspoon baking powder, sifted

1 teaspoon baking soda, sifted

1 teaspoon ground cinnamon

½ cup buttermilk, at room temperature

¼ cup brewed espresso

Honey Whipped Cream (recipe follows)

Chocolate Icing (recipe follows)

1. Preheat the oven to 350°F. Generously butter a 9-inch square or round baking pan.

2. Place the chocolate in a small bowl and set the bowl in a saucepan of gently simmering water. Allow the chocolate to slowly melt. Do not get any water in the chocolate or it will get grainy. Slightly cool the melted chocolate.

3. In the large bowl of a stand mixer, beat the butter and brown sugar for about 5 minutes, or until light and fluffy. Gradually beat in the honey until well blended. Add the eggs one at a time, beating well after each addition. Add the vanilla. Blend in the chocolate.

4. Sift the flour, baking powder, baking soda, and cinnamon. Combine the buttermilk and espresso in a separate bowl.

5. With a rubber spatula, alternately add the dry ingredients and the buttermilk mixture to the creamed mixture. Blend well.

6. Spread the batter in the pan. Bake for about 45 minutes, or until the edges pull away from the sides and a thin skewer or cake tester inserted in the center comes out clean. When the cake is cooled, cut it into squares or rectangles and top each with a mound of stiffly beaten Honey Whipped Cream. Or, if making the cake in a round pan, turn the cake out of the pan and spread Chocolate Icing along the sides and on top of the cake.

Variations:

HONEY WHIPPED CREAM: Whip 1 cup of heavy cream until soft peaks begin to form. Gradually beat in 2 tablespoons of honey and 1 teaspoon of vanilla extract. Beat until the cream makes stiff peaks.

CHOCOLATE ICING: Heat 1 cup of heavy cream, 8 ounces of coarsely chopped semisweet chocolate, and ⅓ cup of honey in a heavy medium-size saucepan. Cook, stirring constantly, for about 2 minutes, or until simmering and smooth. Add 2 tablespoons of cold butter and stir until melted. Refrigerate, stirring every 30 minutes, until the mixture is of icing consistency and stiff enough to spread.

Typically in sweet baked goods I reach for mildly flavored honey such as clover, orange, and alfalfa. But in this recipe I've had favorable results using more robust amber or brown honeys such as buckwheat, mesquite, or wildflower.

micki's special honey fudge brownies

Makes 16 squares

I first ate Micki Weinberg's honey-laced brownies at a honey tasting I hosted for a small group of San Francisco Professional Food Society members. After the tasting we enjoyed a buffet of dishes, and we devoured these special brownies, even after a two-hour tasting of a dozen honey varieties. Micki graciously agreed to let me include her recipe in my book.

4 squares (4 ounces) unsweetened baking chocolate

½ cup (1 stick) unsalted butter

1 cup honey

3 large eggs, at room temperature

1 teaspoon vanilla extract

½ teaspoon coarse salt

⅔ cup all-purpose flour

1 teaspoon baking powder

1 cup coarsely chopped walnuts

1. Preheat the oven to 325°F. Lightly butter a 9-inch square pan, or line the inside with aluminum foil.

2. Place the chocolate and butter in a heavy saucepan and melt over very low heat for about 1 minute, stirring often. Or, if preferred, put the chocolate and butter in a bowl and melt in a microwave on medium power, stirring every 30 seconds, until smooth and the chocolate is melted.

$3.$ Place the chocolate mixture in the large bowl of a stand mixer and gradually beat in the honey, scraping down the sides with a rubber spatula as needed. Add the eggs, one at a time, beating well after each addition. Beat in the vanilla and salt.

$4.$ Sift the flour and baking powder. Add the mixture to the batter and beat on low speed until blended. Add the walnuts and fold them into the batter with a rubber spatula.

$5.$ Spread the batter in the pan. Bake for about 40 minutes, or until the top is set and the sides pull away from the pan. For fudgy brownies, remove from the oven 5 minutes sooner. A toothpick inserted in the center will test moist. Let cool in the pan and cut into squares.

{ **TYPE** OF **HONEY** } *Because the heat of the oven neutralizes the subtle flavor notes in varietal honey, I prefer to make this loaf with a mild honey such as alfalfa, clover, or orange blossom.*

ginger honey walnut loaf

Makes one 9 by 5-inch loaf

My love for ginger inspired this easy recipe, which is more cake than bread. Don't be shocked by the amount of ground ginger in the batter. Its heat and spice help balance the sweetness of the honey, ultimately asserting itself as the dominant flavor. Serve the loaf at room temperature the day it is baked, or refrigerate and serve toasted with a drizzle of honey for as long as the loaf lasts.

½ cup (1 stick) unsalted butter, at room temperature

½ cup firmly packed light brown sugar

½ cup honey

2 large eggs, at room temperature

1 teaspoon vanilla extract

2 cups unbleached all-purpose flour

2 teaspoons baking powder, sifted

½ teaspoon baking soda, sifted

1 tablespoon ground ginger

1 teaspoon ground cinnamon

½ teaspoon coarse salt

½ cup milk (2 percent)

½ cup finely chopped walnuts

1. Preheat the oven to 350°F. Butter a 9 by 5-inch loaf pan. Line the bottom with a piece of buttered waxed paper or parchment paper cut to fit.

2. Place the butter and brown sugar in the large bowl of a stand mixer and beat for about 5 minutes, or until light and fluffy. Gradually add the honey and beat until light, scraping the sides and bottom of the bowl once or twice. Add the eggs one at a time, beating after each addition until light. Beat in the vanilla.

3. Combine the flour, baking powder, baking soda, ginger, cinnamon, and salt in a bowl. On the lowest speed of the mixer, gradually beat the flour mixture into the batter until blended. Gradually add the milk on the lowest speed. Stir in the walnuts with a rubber spatula.

4. Spoon into the pan, smooth the surface with the spatula, and bake for 35 to 40 minutes, until the loaf is golden on top, the edges are lightly browned, and a tester inserted in the center comes out clean. Let cool in the pan before removing. Serve slices plain or toasted and buttered.

Mead, also called honey wine, is made by fermenting honey and water that sometimes is flavored by fruit or spices. Dating from antiquity, mead has made a comeback in recent years, with websites and books describing how to make artisanal mead and mead bars gaining in popularity.

Use any lightly flavored honey such as alfalfa, clover, or orange blossom, although the big spicy flavors in this cake stand up well to a dark, complex-tasting buckwheat, sourwood, mesquite, or other amber or brown honey.

apple, pecan, and honey spice cake

Makes one 10-inch Bundt cake, about 10 servings

Chunky with apples and pecans and laced with the robust flavor of a dark amber buckwheat or late-summer wildflower honey, this cake is wildly popular. It'll keep for several days if wrapped tightly in aluminum foil.

3 large eggs, at room temperature

¾ cup firmly packed light brown sugar

2 teaspoons vanilla extract

¾ cup honey

¾ cup flavorless vegetable oil

2½ cups unbleached all-purpose flour

2 teaspoons ground cinnamon

1 teaspoon baking powder, sifted

1 teaspoon baking soda, sifted

½ teaspoon coarse salt

3 cups peeled, cored, and diced crisp apples (Fuji, Granny Smith, or Golden Delicious)

1 cup chopped pecans

1. Preheat the oven to 325°F. Generously coat a 10-inch Bundt pan with butter or nonstick cooking spray.

2. Place the eggs, brown sugar, and vanilla in the large bowl of a stand mixer and beat for 5 minutes, until light and fluffy. Add the honey in a slow drizzle, constantly beating until well blended. Beat in the oil using the same slow drizzle method.

3. In a separate bowl, combine the flour, cinnamon, baking powder, baking soda, and salt. Add the flour mixture, apples, and pecans to the batter and stir with a wooden spoon or rubber spatula until thoroughly incorporated.

4. Spoon into the pan and smooth the surface with a spatula. Bake for 1 hour and 10 minutes, until the edges are browned and pulling away from the sides and a toothpick inserted in the center comes out clean.

I prefer a mildly sweet orange or lemon blossom honey for this recipe.

sweet cheese tart

Makes one 9-inch tart, 6 to 8 servings

This is a dainty version of cheesecake but with the slightly grainy texture of ricotta, the essence of your favorite honey, and the bright taste of orange zest. The crust is a cookie dough that is quickly made in a food processor and pressed into a tart pan. No painstaking rolling-out of dough is required.

1 tablespoon melted unsalted butter

Butter Crust

1½ cups all-purpose flour

3 tablespoons sugar

Pinch of coarse salt

½ cup (1 stick) cold unsalted butter, cut into small pieces

1 egg yolk, at room temperature

1 teaspoon vanilla extract

Tart Filling

1 cup whole-milk ricotta cheese, at room temperature (see note)

4 ounces cream cheese, softened

1 large egg, warmed (see page 137)

½ cup honey

2 tablespoons all-purpose flour

1 teaspoon grated orange zest

1 teaspoon vanilla extract

Honey Lemon Sauce (page 155) or Dried Sour Cherry Honey Sauce (page 54), for serving

1. Preheat the oven to 350°F.

2. Lightly coat the bottom and sides of a 9-inch tart pan with removable bottom or a springform pan with the melted butter. Place the flour, sugar, and salt in the bowl of a food processor. Pulse just to combine. Add the cold butter a few pieces at a time, pulsing until each addition is incorporated and the mixture is the consistency of sand.

continued on page 154

3. In a small bowl stir the egg yolk and vanilla until blended. Add to the flour and butter mixture and pulse repeatedly until the mixture gathers into a soft pastry dough. Do not under process or the dough will be too crumbly. This can take up to 1 minute, so be patient.

4. Remove the blade from the food processor. Turn the dough onto a lightly floured board and lightly press into a rounded disk. Put the dough in the pan and with floured fingers gently press it along the bottom and up the sides of the pan. It does not have to be a smooth surface.

5. To make the filling, combine the ricotta, cream cheese, egg, honey, flour, orange zest, and vanilla in the bowl of a food processor or a blender and process until smooth. Pour the mixture into the crust.

6. Bake the tart for about 45 minutes, or until the filling is firm and the crust is golden. Let cool on a wire rack. The tart is delicious served warm or cold with Honey Lemon Sauce (page 155) or Dried Sour Cherry Honey Sauce (page 54).

Note: *Some ricotta brands have a drier texture than others. If the ricotta you are using is not creamy, process or blend it with 1 to 2 tablespoons of milk or cream until the consistency is creamier.*

I prefer the subtle, sweet, and floral notes of an orange blossom or clover honey in this simple sauce.

honey lemon sauce

Makes about 3 cups

This recipe is adapted from a family favorite used with warm gingerbread. The original recipe uses lots of sugar, but in this interesting twist the honey gives it a cleaner, fresher lemon taste. I use thin-skinned, mildly tart Meyer lemons for the sauce because I live where Meyer lemons grow in the backyard. If you're using thicker-skinned lemons that are more sour, decrease the amount of lemon juice to ¼ cup. Serve this sauce over slices of Ginger Honey Walnut Loaf (page 150) or Sweet Cheese Tart (page 153), or over a plain chiffon, pound, or angel food cake.

2 cups water

¼ cup cornstarch

Pinch of coarse salt

¾ cup orange blossom or clover honey

½ cup fresh Meyer lemon juice, or ⅓ cup juice from other lemons

2 teaspoons grated lemon zest

1 lemon, seeded and cut into paper-thin slices

1. In a saucepan, combine ½ cup of the water and cornstarch, whisking until there are no lumps. Add the remaining 1½ cups water and heat over medium heat, stirring gently until the mixture begins to boil and thicken. Add the salt, honey, lemon juice, and grated zest. Cook for 1 to 2 minutes. Add the lemon slices.

2. Taste and add more lemon juice or honey if desired. Serve warm over the cake. The sauce will keep for about 1 week in a tightly lidded container and refrigerated. Reheat before serving.

honey pear tart

Makes 1 (9-inch) tart, about 6 servings

Make this delightful tart with whatever fruit is in season. In the summer I use blueberries, raspberries, peaches, or figs, but the rest of the year I use pears. Almost any variety of pear can be used. Pears are one of the few fruits that should be picked unripe and allowed to ripen at room temperature.

Tart

¼ cup raisins

¼ cup brandy

1 tablespoon melted butter

Butter Crust

1½ cups unbleached all-purpose flour

2 tablespoons sugar

½ teaspoon coarse salt

½ cup (1 stick) cold unsalted butter, cut into ¼-inch pieces

1 egg yolk

1 teaspoon vanilla extract

Pear Filling

4 ripe pears (any variety), peeled, cored, quartered, and thinly sliced

1 tablespoon all-purpose flour

½ teaspoon freshly grated nutmeg or ground cinnamon

4 tablespoons honey

Earl's Honey Butter Sauce (page 158)

1. Preheat the oven to 450°F.

2. About 1 hour before baking the tart, place the raisins and brandy in a small saucepan and warm, stirring, over low heat. When hot, remove from the heat, cover, and let stand for about 1 hour, or until the brandy is absorbed. Pour off excess brandy, if any, and reserve for other use.

3. Use the melted butter to lightly coat the bottom and sides of a 9-inch tart pan with removable bottom or a springform pan.

4. To make the crust, combine the flour, sugar, and salt in the bowl of a food processor. Pulse just to combine. Add the cold butter a few pieces at a time, pulsing until each addition is incorporated and the mixture is the consistency of sand.

5. In a small bowl, stir the egg yolk and vanilla until blended. Add to the flour and butter mixture and pulse repeatedly until the mixture gathers into a soft dough. Do not under-process or the dough will be too crumbly. This can take up to 1 minute, so be patient.

6. Remove the blade from the food processor. Turn the dough onto a lightly floured board and lightly press into a rounded disk. Put the dough in the pan and with floured fingers gently press it along the bottom and up the sides of the pan. It does not have to be a smooth surface.

7. To make the filling, combine the pears, flour, and nutmeg in a bowl and gently toss to coat. Drizzle with the honey and add the soaked raisins; toss just to blend.

8. Spread the fruit over the dough in an even layer, arranging the top layer of pear slices in an attractive spiral. Place the raisins strategically between the pear slices.

9. Bake for 15 minutes. Reduce the oven temperature to 350°F and bake for about 35 minutes more, or until the edges are golden brown.

10. Slice the tart and swirl a bit of Earl's Honey Butter Sauce over each slice.

For this recipe I prefer to use E.G. Flewellen's Midsummer Wildflower Honey, a heady blend of wildflowers with a pronounced hint of fennel, which blankets the hills of Port Costa, California, throughout the season. But feel free to use almost any favorite honey with a mix of wildflower or fruit blossom nectars.

earl's honey butter sauce

Makes about ¾ cup

Earl Flewellen, beekeeper extraordinaire and proprietor with his partner, Samuel, of the Honey House Café in Port Costa, California, generously shared this wonderfully simple but oh-so-luscious sauce to serve over any number of delicious cakes. At the Honey House Café, located in the historic Burlington Hotel, the sauce is spooned over wedges of warm cornbread and thick slices of moist pound cake. It is equally delicious served on ice cream, gingerbread, spice cake, and chocolate cake. I use it as a decadent drizzle on Honey Pear Tart. Although the honey isn't caramelized, Earl calls this his caramel sauce.

½ cup honey

¼ cup (½ stick) cold salted butter,
cut into ½-inch pieces

Gently heat the honey in a small saucepan over low heat just until warmed. Add the cold butter and stir just until the butter is melted into the honey and makes a smooth sauce. Do not boil. Serve warm.

{ TYPE OF HONEY } *Use a full-flavored dark wildflower, mesquite, sourwood, basswood, or other honey with spicy flavor notes that will marry well with the dry white wine and big flavor profile of the vanilla bean.*

crinkly honey-roasted pears with vanilla

Makes 4 servings

Simple, elegant, and *sublime* are just three of many words to describe these pears. They are incredibly easy to make; no paring or coring is even necessary. Basted with a vanilla-laced mixture of wine and honey while baking, they emerge from the oven glistening with crinkled skin. The pear flesh melts in your mouth.

1 cup dry white wine	2 bay leaves
½ cup honey	1 vanilla bean, split down the middle
4 small Bosc pears, preferably with stems attached	Honey Vanilla Yogurt (recipe follows) or crème fraîche (optional)

1. Preheat the oven to 350°F.

2. Place the wine and honey in a small, shallow baking dish or pie plate and whisk until thoroughly blended. Cut a thin slice from the bottom of each pear and stand, stem end up, in the wine mixture. Add the bay leaves and vanilla bean to the dish.

3. Bake for about 60 minutes, or until the pears are crinkly and tender when pierced with a toothpick or skewer. Baste with the wine mixture every 20 minutes while baking.

4. To serve, place each pear in a shallow soup plate with room for the wine syrup to be spooned over the top. Serve warm or at room temperature, topped with a spoonful of Honey Vanilla Yogurt or crème fraîche.

Honey Vanilla Yogurt:
In a small bowl, stir together ½ cup of plain, low-fat Greek yogurt, 2 tablespoons of honey (the same variety used in the baked pears), and ½ teaspoon of vanilla extract.

If possible match the honey with the thyme or rosemary used in the dish. Or use any bright, fresh lemon or orange blossom, star thistle, lavender, or other honey.

roasted honey-glazed figs with herbed goat cheese on fig leaves

Makes 6 servings

A pretty dish of halved figs roasted with goat cheese and drizzled with honey makes a delicious summer appetizer or dessert. If you have access to big, beautiful leaves, picked fresh off a nearby fig tree, use them to line the baking dish. When food is cooked on top of or wrapped in fig leaves, it takes on an intriguing taste best described as coconut or cinnamon. If fresh figs are not available, try this with halved ripe apricots. It's equally delicious and stunningly photogenic.

Extra-virgin olive oil, for the baking dish, plus 1 tablespoon

1 large fresh fig leaf or 2 medium-size fig leaves, stems trimmed (optional)

6 large ripe figs, stem ends trimmed, halved lengthwise

6 ounces fresh goat cheese, cut from a log and into ½-inch chunks

1 tablespoon fresh thyme or rosemary leaves

3 tablespoons honey

Coarse salt and freshly ground black pepper

Approximately ½ teaspoon aged balsamic vinegar

1 baguette, warmed and sliced

1. Preheat the oven to 450°F. Lightly brush a pie plate or 8-inch gratin or other shallow baking dish with a thin film of olive oil. Place the fig leaves in the dish, covering the bottom.

2. Arrange the figs, cut side up, around the outside edges of the dish. Arrange the cheese chunks in a single layer in the center. Sprinkle the figs and cheese with the thyme. Drizzle the figs and cheese lightly with the honey and 1 tablespoon of olive oil. Season the cheese and figs with the salt and pepper.

3. Roast for about 15 minutes, or until the fig leaf begins to curl and the cheese and figs soften.

4. Before serving, carefully place a tiny drop of the vinegar in the center of each fig. To serve, present a basket of sliced baguette. Spread each slice with the softened cheese and top with a fig half.

{ TYPE OF HONEY } *I like either a delicate floral honey such as tupelo or orange blossom, or saguaro, mesquite, or star thistle with distinctively spicy notes that will stand up to the ginger.*

honey, mango, orange, and ginger sorbet

Makes 4 servings

I adore mangoes so much I once went all the way to India, home of the lusciously fragrant, silken Alphonso mango, to attend a mango festival. Fortunately, in the United States we can get quite good mangoes from California and Mexico. For this dish, buy round mangoes with leathery red, green, and orange mottled skin. They are the least stringy.

2 large ripe mangoes, peeled, seeded, and cubed (about 3 cups)

1½ cups fresh orange juice

⅓ cup honey

¼ cup fresh lime juice

1 tablespoon coarsely chopped ginger

1. Combine the mangoes, orange juice, honey, lime juice, and ginger in a food processor and pulse repeatedly until the mixture is evenly smooth.

2. If you have an ice-cream maker, freeze the sorbet according to the manufacturer's directions. Or transfer the mixture to a shallow 9 by 13-inch baking pan and freeze for 2 hours, stirring from time to time; when almost firm, break it into chunks and process in a food processor until smooth. Pack the sorbet into a quart container and freeze until ready to serve.

{ TYPE OF HONEY } *Almost any honey you have on hand will work in this recipe. I like orange blossom, alfalfa, or wildflower.*

honey and cardamom oven-baked chunky rhubarb

Makes 4 servings

My first experience cooking rhubarb resulted in a stringy mass in a saucepan. I loved the taste but not the texture. Then I discovered oven-baked rhubarb. If you can avoid stirring, the rhubarb will slowly poach in its own juices with a bit of sweetening, in this case honey. The cardamom is a twist on the typical seasonings of vanilla bean, a cinnamon stick, or slices of raw ginger.

¼ teaspoon cardamom seeds (from about 8 pods)

1 pound rhubarb, trimmed and cut into 1-inch pieces (about 3½ cups)

⅓ cup honey

¼ cup water

1 strip (½ by 3 inches) orange zest, twisted to release flavor

Heavy cream, plain or vanilla yogurt, or vanilla ice cream

1. Preheat the oven to 350°F. Break up the cardamom seeds with a mortar and pestle and place in a deep, 2-quart baking dish, preferably with a lid. Add the rhubarb and drizzle with the honey and water. Add the orange zest.

2. Bake, covered with a lid or tightly covered with aluminum foil, for 20 to 25 minutes, until the rhubarb is tender. Do not stir, or the rhubarb will become stringy. Let cool and serve with a drizzle of the heavy cream or a spoonful of the yogurt or ice cream.

I prefer a complex wildflower honey with fennel blossom and herbal notes. But use any full-bodied honey you have on hand. You will not be disappointed.

honey and almond butter ice cream

Makes about 1½ pints

The almond butter and honey are perfect companions in this rich ice cream. To add more crunch and a hit of roasted almond flavor, sprinkle each serving with chopped toasted almonds.

1½ cups whole milk

1 cup heavy cream

4 egg yolks

⅔ cup honey

½ cup smooth or chunky almond butter

⅛ teaspoon almond extract

1. Place the milk, cream, and egg yolks in a heavy saucepan. Slowly whisk to combine. Cook over low heat, stirring gently, for about 5 minutes, or until the milk is hot and the mixture begins to coat a spoon. If you don't have a heavy saucepan, use a double boiler so the egg yolks do not curdle. Remove from the heat.

2. Add the honey, almond butter, and almond extract and stir until thoroughly blended. Refrigerate, uncovered, until chilled.

3. Following the manufacturer's directions, process the custard in an ice-cream maker. Scoop the ice cream into a freezer container and freeze until ready to serve. It will keep for at least 2 weeks.

I prefer a deep flavored amber-hued honey that will stand up to the rich ice cream. My choices include wildflower with a heady floral aroma and flavor with hints of fennel, a richly floral sunflower honey with hints of vanilla, a spicy golden rod honey or a buttery avocado honey.

honey-almond ripple ice cream in a jiffy

Makes about 1½ pints

Not in the mood to make a custard? Consider this alternative.

½ cup whole almonds, skins on

1¾ cups honey

1 pint good-quality vanilla ice cream

1. Spread the almonds in a small baking dish and toast in the oven at 350°F for 15 minutes. Let cool and chop coarsely. Combine the almonds and honey in a pint jar and set aside.

2. Scoop the ice cream into a bowl and break up with the side of a large spoon. Spoon about ½ cup of the honey and almonds on top and quickly fold once or twice to form honey-almond ripples in the ice cream. Quickly repack into the ice-cream carton and freeze until firm.

3. To serve, scoop the ice cream into bowls and top with spoonfuls of the remaining honey-almond mixture.

warm pear and apple sauce with honey and nutmeg

Makes 6 cups

Homemade apple or pear sauce is among the simplest of all recipes. Make this with all apples, all pears, or a mixture of the two, using different varieties of fruits depending on what is on hand.

2 to 3 pounds apples, any variety, in various stages of ripeness

2 to 3 pounds pears, any variety, in various stages of ripeness

¼ cup fresh lemon juice

2 tablespoons honey, or more to taste

½ teaspoon grated nutmeg, or more to taste

1. Quarter the fruit and remove the cores and stems. Place the pieces in a large (7- to 8-quart), heavy enameled cast-iron or similar pan. Add the lemon juice and set over medium-low heat. Cover and heat, stirring occasionally, just until the mixture begins to steam. Stir well.

2. Cover and cook over low heat for 20 to 30 minutes, until the fruit is cooked down and mushy. The cooking time will depend on the ripeness of the fruit. Let stand, covered, for about 20 minutes, or until slightly cool.

3. Set a food mill over a large, deep bowl. Working in batches, puree the fruit through the mill. When peels back up on the strainer, remove with a spoon and discard. Scrape the pureed sauce from under the strainer and add to the bowl. Repeat until all of the cooked fruit pieces are pureed into the bowl.

4. Add the honey and nutmeg. Taste and adjust the seasonings as needed.

5. Serve cold with yogurt and a drizzle of additional honey, or serve warm with a scoop of Honey and Almond Butter Ice Cream (page 166) and a ladleful of Earl's Honey Butter Sauce (page 158).

Here you must use a favorite honey. My first test was with a fireweed honey from Colorado. The flavor of the honey sings as a soprano. The wine is the chorus. The zabaglione is the opera. Subsequent tests were made with a favorite rich Northern California wildflower honey, French lavender, and a minty Sicilian lemon blossom.

honey zabaglione

Makes 4 servings

This is one experiment that far surpassed my expectations: honey in a classic zabaglione recipe as a substitute for sugar. The servings are small because this rich cream is half pudding and half confection. In other words, a little goes a long way. Serve in stemmed wineglasses, small sherry glasses, or espresso cups with small spoons so each taste can be savored. It is also lovely served as a topping over fresh berries or sliced fruit.

¼ cup honey

4 large egg yolks, at room temperature

¼ cup floral white wine such as chardonnay or pinot grigio

Fresh berries, for garnish

1. Measure the honey in a glass cup. Place the cup in a heatproof bowl and carefully add very hot water to the bowl. Let the honey stand until it is warmed and thinned.

2. Put the egg yolks in the top of a double boiler or in a heatproof bowl that will fit snugly over a larger pan. Place on a folded dish towel and beat the yolks with a whisk or handheld mixer for about 5 minutes, or until pale yellow. Drizzle in the honey, continuing to beat constantly. Beat in the wine.

3. Put about 1 inch of water in the bottom part of the double boiler or a saucepan and heat to simmering. Decrease the heat to low. Put the top of the double boiler or the heatproof bowl over the simmering water and beat the zabaglione with a wire whisk for at least 7 minutes, until thick and foamy. Pour into stemmed wineglasses, garnish with berries, and serve at once.

Panna cotta is the perfect canvas for your most delicious and precious honey. I like a mild, not overly sweet honey with floral notes such as orange or lemon blossom, lavender, star thistle, tupelo, or fireweed.

honey panna cotta

Makes 4 to 6 servings

At a favorite Italian restaurant, I was once served a delicately set panna cotta spooned onto a large plate. A departure from the typical pudding cup serving, this is how I've been serving this simple dessert ever since. If preferred, the panna cotta can be made in individual pudding dishes or ramekins. However, I like the spooned version because it allows a large surface for a drizzle of honey to cascade in narrow rivulets down the sides of the pudding.

1 cup half-and-half

1 cup heavy cream

3 whole cloves

2 cinnamon sticks

1 strip orange zest

2 tablespoons water

2 teaspoons unflavored gelatin

¼ cup honey, plus more for serving

Honey-Sweetened Fruit
(recipe follows), for serving

1. Place the half-and-half, cream, cloves, cinnamon sticks, and orange zest in a medium saucepan and heat over medium-low, stirring constantly, until small bubbles appear around the edges. Cover and let stand off the heat for 15 minutes.

2. Place 2 tablespoons of water in a small bowl or cup and sprinkle the gelatin evenly on the surface. Let stand for about 5 minutes, or until softened.

3. Lift the solids (spices and zest) from the warm cream mixture with a slotted spoon. Add the honey and softened gelatin to the cream mixture and stir gently until the gelatin is dissolved.

4. Pour into a shallow bowl, cover, and refrigerate for 2 to 3 hours, until set. For a delicate texture, serve panna cotta the same day. As it stands the texture will stiffen slightly.

continued on page 172

5. To serve, place a large spoon of panna cotta on a dessert plate and drizzle with about 1 tablespoon of honey. Surround with sliced peaches, strawberries, or Honey-Sweetened Fruit.

Honey-Sweetened Fruit

Combine 1 to 2 cups of sliced strawberries; a mixture of sliced strawberries, blueberries, and raspberries; or peeled and sliced ripe peaches or nectarines with 1 tablespoon of honey. Gently fold to blend and let stand at room temperature until ready to serve.

Use a full-flavored, amber-hued honey such as eucalyptus, Christmas Berry (from Australia), buckwheat, mesquite, leatherwood, pumpkin blossom, or whatever you have on hand. Select a honey that has menthol, mint, vanilla, or spice flavor notes that seem to bring out the best in chocolate.

velvety honey-chocolate pudding

Makes 4 to 6 servings

For some reason, chocolate emphasizes the distinctive flavor notes in full-bodied honey. It is one of those pleasant yet mysterious taste sensations. This pudding is a family favorite and is one of the first recipes I teach my grandkids to make. It's a winner every time.

¼ cup unsweetened cocoa powder

3 tablespoons cornstarch

1½ cups milk

½ cup heavy cream

¼ cup honey

2 squares (2 ounces) semisweet chocolate, chopped

1 teaspoon vanilla extract

1. Place the cocoa and cornstarch in a medium saucepan and whisk until completely blended.

2. In a separate saucepan on medium heat, or in a 1-quart glass measuring cup in the microwave, heat the milk, cream, and honey until warmed. Stir to blend. Slowly whisk the milk mixture into the cocoa mixture until the cocoa and cornstarch are dissolved and the mixture is smooth. Heat over medium heat, stirring gently with a rubber spatula, until the mixture begins to thicken.

3. Add the chopped chocolate and boil gently, stirring for about 1 minute, or until the chocolate melts. Remove from the heat. Let stand for 5 minutes and then stir in the vanilla.

4. Pour into a serving bowl or individual pudding cups and refrigerate until slightly chilled or cold.

My favorite honey for this is a richly floral type created with the nectar of lavender flowers. Orange or lemon blossom, tupelo, acacia, star thistle, raspberry, and blackberry are also good choices.

honey ricotta pudding

Makes 4 to 6 servings

Don't be fooled into thinking that such a simple recipe isn't elegant or sophisticated, because it is. Splurge on a high-quality, freshly made artisanal ricotta, if available. There are only three primary ingredients in this recipe, and at least two of them—the ricotta and the honey—must be first rate.

1½ cups (about 6 ounces) ricotta

¼ cup confectioners' sugar

¼ cup honey, plus more for serving

2 tablespoons heavy cream (optional)

Dried Sour Cherry Honey Sauce (page 54) or Honey and Fresh Fruit Sauce (page 177)

1. Combine the ricotta, sugar, and honey in the bowl of a food processor. Pulse for at least 1 minute, until the mixture is well combined and very smooth and fluffy. If the ricotta mixture is dry, add the cream and process until creamy.

2. Remove the metal blade and scrape the ricotta mixture into a bowl. Cover and refrigerate for at least 1 hour before serving. The pudding will keep for 3 days.

3. To serve, spoon into small bowls. Drizzle with the same honey used to flavor the pudding, or top with Dried Sour Cherry Honey Sauce or Honey and Fresh Fruit Sauce.

For these fragile cakes I like to use a golden honey with light floral notes such as orange blossom, star thistle, or tupelo.

nana's honey cakes

Makes 4 servings

Spanning four generations now I have seen pyramids of these cakes glistening with honey and sitting on a sideboard in honor of Christmas, Easter, and other family celebrations. An honored tradition in our family, Nana's Honey Cakes take several pairs of hands to readily make. The production involves making egg dough, rolling and cutting it into narrow ribbons, pinching the ribbons into spirals (or "rosettes" as my grandmother, Nana, called them), frying them in oil, and dipping them in honey. Nana's crowning glory was colored sprinkles—for the kids—but I tend to not use them. Although some things change over generations, Nana's Honey Cakes are still with us.

Dough

3 to 4 cups unbleached all-purpose flour

1 tablespoon sugar

1 teaspoon baking powder, sifted

½ teaspoon coarse salt

5 eggs, at room temperature

1 tablespoon olive oil

2 quarts vegetable oil, for frying

3 to 4 cups honey, for dipping

1. Combine 3 cups of the flour, sugar, baking powder, and salt in a large bowl. Beat the eggs and olive oil in a smaller bowl until well blended. Using a wooden spoon, gradually stir the eggs into the flour until the mixture is too stiff to stir.

2. Turn the stiff dough out onto a board generously floured with some of the remaining flour. Knead the flour into the dough, adding the rest of the flour as needed (and more if the dough is still sticky), for about 10 minutes, or until the dough is smooth and pliable. (You can do this with the dough hook on a mixer, if necessary.) To test whether the dough is ready, cut it in half and look for small bubbles throughout. If the dough is sticky inside, sprinkle with more flour and knead for a minute or two longer. Cover the dough with a folded dish towel and let it rest for 20 to 30 minutes.

continued on page 176

3. Divide the dough evenly into 8 pieces. Working with one piece at a time, flatten the dough on the board into an oval. Feed the dough into a pasta rolling machine beginning on the widest setting (number 1). When the dough emerges, fold it in half and re-roll. If the dough sticks to the machine, dust it with flour and re-roll. Proceed with the rolling of the same piece of dough (for subsequent rolling, do not fold the dough). Roll the dough through each setting on the knob from 2 through 6, until it emerges as a long, wide, thin ribbon. Depending on the size of the ovals, each ribbon of dough should be 15 to 18 inches long and 3 to 4 inches wide. Lay the ribbons out on a lightly floured surface. Using a knife, trim the uneven edges into straight lines and then cut the dough lengthwise into long ribbons 1½ to 2 inches wide.

4. To shape the dough, set out a small bowl of water for dampening your fingers. Form the strips of dough into spirals, pinching with dampened fingertips every inch or so to keep them together while frying.

5. Meanwhile, half-fill a heavy large 6- to 8-quart Dutch oven with the vegetable oil and heat to about 350°F, or until hot enough to lightly brown a crust of bread. Set out sheet pans topped with large wire racks for cooling the fried honey cakes.

6. When the oil is heated, fry the honey cakes 2 or 3 at a time, 2 to 3 minutes, turning gently with tongs until golden. Transfer to the wire racks and continue until all of the honey cakes are fried.

7. In a deep, narrow 3-quart saucepan, heat the honey, stirring, over low heat just until lukewarm and slightly thinned. Using tongs, dip the honey cakes into the warm honey one at a time. Hold the cakes over the saucepan to allow excess honey to drip away and then put them on the wire racks set over rimmed sheet pans to catch the dripping honey. Continue until all honey cakes have been coated with honey.

8. Pile the honey cakes on a large platter. For crisp honey cakes, serve within one or two days. For a more dense, chewy texture, let them stand uncovered for a couple of days. Either way, they are irresistible.

Quick Hits: Sweets

- To make a simple Honey and Fresh Fruit Sauce, add ¼ cup of your favorite honey and 2 tablespoons of lime juice to 3 cups fresh fruit including cut-up ripe peaches, nectarines, or strawberries, and whole blueberries or raspberries.

- Fold a thick, rich avocado, wildflower, or buckwheat honey into semisoftened vanilla or chocolate ice cream for honey ripple ice cream.

- Stir ½ teaspoon of ground cinnamon and ½ teaspoon of vanilla extract into 1 cup of creamy, whole-milk ricotta and drizzle with lemon blossom, star thistle, or blackberry honey. Serve with wedges of fresh figs, ripe pears, peaches, or nectarines.

- Stir ½ teaspoon of grated orange or lemon zest into 1 cup of creamy, whole-milk ricotta. Sprinkle with ground cinnamon and drizzle with honey.

- To make Toasted Walnuts in Honey, toast 1 cup of walnuts in a 350°F oven for 10 to 12 minutes, until lightly toasted. Stir into 1 cup (12 ounces) of honey and store in a jar until ready to serve. If the mixture is too thick to spoon, warm the jar in a saucepan of hot water. Serve over ice cream, yogurt, cottage cheese, or fruit, or with cheese and fruit.

- To make Toasted Marcona Almonds in Rosemary Honey, combine 1½ cups of honey, 1 cup of roasted and salted Marcona almonds, and 1 tablespoon of finely chopped fresh rosemary in a pint jar. Tightly cover and let stand in a sunny spot for 2 days, turning the jar over at least twice. Do not refrigerate. Serve over ice cream or with cheese and fruit.

- Beat 1 cup of heavy cream with 3 tablespoons of your favorite honey and 1 teaspoon of vanilla extract until of desired consistency. Use to top chocolate or other pudding, pumpkin or other pie, or pound or any uniced cake or cupcakes.

- Make cream cheese frosting with one 8-ounce package of softened cream cheese and ¼ cup of honey beaten until smooth.

Bibliography

Berenbaum, May. *Honey, I'm Homemade*. Chicago: University of Illinois Press, 2010.

Carpenter, Novella, and Rosenthal, Willow. *The Essential Urban Farmer*. New York: Penguin, 2011.

Ellison, Virginia H. *The Pooh Cook Book*. New York: E. P. Dutton, 1969.

Havenhand, Gloria. *Honey: Nature's Golden Healer*. Buffalo, NY: Firefly Books, 2010.

Jacobsen, Rowan. *Fruitless Fall*. New York: Bloomsbury USA. 2008

McGee, Harold. *On Food and Cooking*. New York: Scribner, 1984.

Mellor, Isha. *Honey*. New York: Congdon & Lattès, 1981.

Nordhaus, Hannah. *The Beekeeper's Lament*. New York: Harper Perennial, 2011.

Norman, Jill. *Honey*. New York: Bantam Books, 1991.

Rosenbaum, Stephanie. *Honey: From Flower to Table*. San Francisco: Chronicle, 2002.

Style, Sue. *Honey: From Hive to Honeypot*. San Francisco: Chronicle, 1993.

Toussaint-Samat, Maguelonne. *History of Food*. Oxford UK: Blackwell Publishers, 1992.

Upton, Gene. *Honey: A Connoisseur's Guide with Recipes*. Berkeley, CA, and Toronto: Ten Speed Press, 2000.

Sources

Information on Honey

www.rmiucdavis.edu
The Robert Mondavi Institute for Wine and Food Science at the University of California, Davis, offers programs on bees, honey, and pollination.

www.vanishingbees.com
This site is dedicated to a film that looks at the possible causes for the frightening phenomenon of colony collapse disorder.

www.honey.com
This is a National Honey Board resource for U.S. honey, honey production, and news on bees. At www.honeylocator.com, the board has a guide to finding local sources and specific varietals.

www.honeytraveler.com
This offers excellent descriptions of the origins of single-varietal honeys worldwide.

www.benefits-of-honey.com
Honey products and information on medicinal and cosmetic uses for honey can be found.

www.ebeehoney.com
This is a source for information and honey products from raw honey to pollen to propolis cream.

www.gotmead.com
This is one of several sites following the recent interest in making mead.

www.whitehouse.gov/blog/2012/09/01/ale-chief-white-house-beer-recipe
Recipes are available for the White House Honey Ale and White House Honey Porter.

Shopping for Honey

These are only a few of the many honey sources on the Web. My suggestion is to first look for local producers at farmers' markets, natural food stores, and specialty food shops. Then search the Internet for honey from other regions.

www.purelyorganic.com
www.thebeefolks.com
These are excellent sources for interesting honey varietals.

www.spanishtable.com
The Spanish Table is a source for honey imported from Spain, specifically Oak Blossom Honey from Catalonia.

www.redbee.com
Shop for Red Bee's single-origin artisanal honeys, find honey-tasting events, and more.

www.marshallshoney.com
This long-established California producer has many outstanding varietal honeys.

www.katzandco.com
Katz produces Branches Honey, an excellent artisanal product, and a delicious honey vinegar.

www.savannahbeecompany.com
Fine Southern honeys are available from a long-established company.

www.markethallfoods.com
Market Hall is an excellent resource for honeys from Italy, Australia, New Zealand, and more.

www.slideridge.com
Slide Ridge sells delicious honey vinegar, honey wine, and raw honey.

Metric Conversions and Equivalents

Metric Conversion Formulas

To convert	Multiply
Ounces to grams	Ounces by 28.35
Pounds to kilograms	Pounds by 0.454
Teaspoons to milliliters	Teaspoons by 4.93
Tablespoons to milliliters	Tablespoons by 14.79
Fluid ounces to milliliters	Fluid ounces by 29.57
Cups to milliliters	Cups by 236.59
Cups to liters	Cups by 0.236
Quarts to liters	Quarts by 0.946
Inches to centimeters	Inches by 2.54

Approximate Metric Equivalents

Volume

¼ teaspoon	1 milliliter
½ teaspoon	2.5 milliliters
¾ teaspoon	4 milliliters
1 teaspoon	5 milliliters
1 tablespoon (½ fluid ounce)	15 milliliters
¼ cup	60 milliliters
⅓ cup	80 milliliters
½ cup (4 fluid ounces)	120 milliliters
⅔ cup	160 milliliters
¾ cup	180 milliliters
1 cup (8 fluid ounces)	240 milliliters
2 cups (1 pint)	460 milliliters
3 cups	700 milliliters

Weight

1 ounce	28 grams
2 ounces	57 grams
4 ounces (¼ pound)	113 grams
5 ounces	142 grams
6 ounces	170 grams
7 ounces	198 grams
8 ounces (½ pound)	227 grams
16 ounces (1 pound)	454 grams

Length

¼ inch	6 millimeters
½ inch	1.25 centimeters
1 inch	2.5 centimeters
4 inches	10 centimeters
6 inches	15.25 centimeters
12 inches (1 foot)	30 centimeters

Oven Temperatures

To convert Fahrenheit to Celsius, subtract 32 from Fahrenheit, multiply the result by 5, then divide by 9.

description	fahrenheit	celsius	british gas mark
Very cool	200°	95°	0
Very cool	225°	110°	¼
Very cool	250°	120°	½
Cool	275°	135°	1
Cool	300°	150°	2
Warm	325°	165°	3
Moderate	350°	175°	4
Moderately hot	375°	190°	5
Fairly hot	400°	200°	6
Hot	425°	220°	7
Very hot	450°	230°	8
Very hot	475°	245°	9

Common Ingredients and Their Approximate Equivalents

1 cup uncooked rice = 225 grams

1 cup all-purpose flour = 140 grams

1 stick butter (4 ounces • ½ cup • 8 tablespoons) = 110 grams

1 cup butter (8 ounces • 2 sticks • 16 tablespoons) = 220 grams

1 cup brown sugar, firmly packed = 225 grams

1 cup granulated sugar = 200 grams

Information compiled from a variety of sources, including *Recipes into Type* by Joan Whitman and Dolores Simon (Newton, MA: Biscuit Books, 2000); *The New Food Lover's Companion* by Sharon Tyler Herbst (Hauppauge, NY: Barron's, 1995); and *Rosemary Brown's Big Kitchen Instruction Book* (Kansas City, MO: Andrews McMeel, 1998).

Index